Managing in the Public Sector

Sector

A Casebook in Ethics and Leadership

BRETT S. SHARP

University of Central Oklahoma

GRANT AGUIRRE

New Mexico State University

KENNETH KICKHAM

University of Central Oklahoma

Longman

Boston   Columbus   Indianapolis   New York   San Francisco   Upper Saddle River
Amsterdam   Cape Town   Dubai   London   Madrid   Milan   Munich   Paris   Montreal
Toronto   Delhi   Mexico City   São Paulo   Sydney   Hong Kong   Seoul   Singapore   Taipei   Tokyo

Editor-in-Chief: Eric Stano
Editorial Assistant: Elizabeth Alimena
Senior Marketing Manager: Lindsey Prudhomme
Production Manager: Fran Russello
Full Service Project Management: Manjula Mahalingam / PreMediaGlobal
Cover Design Manager: Jayne Conte
Cover Illustration/Photo: © Sergey Ilin / Fotolia
Printer and Binder: Courier Companies, Inc.

Library of Congress Cataloging-in-Publication Data
Sharp, Brett S.
  Managing in the public sector: a casebook in ethics and leadership / Brett S. Sharp,
  Grant Aguirre, Kenneth Kickham.
      p. cm.
  Includes bibliographical references and index.
  ISBN-13: 978-0-13-603975-4 (alk. paper)
  ISBN-10: 0-13-603975-8 (alk. paper)
  1. Public administration—Moral and ethical aspects—United States.
     2. Public administration—Moral and ethical aspects—United States—Case studies.
     I. Aguirre, Grant. II. Kickham, Kenneth. III. Title.
JK468.E7S53 2011
172'.2—dc22
                                                                  2010010693

1 2 3 4 5 6 7 8 9 10—DOH —13 12 11 10

Longman
is an imprint of

www.pearsonhighered.com

ISBN-13: 978-0-13-603975-4
ISBN-10:   0-13-603975-8

Managing in the Public Sector

ONE WEEK LOAN

CONTENTS

CHAPTER 7
Education Administration and Policy   88

CHAPTER 8
To Protect and to Serve   97

CHAPTER 9
Bureaucracy and Public Morality   104

CHAPTER 10
Diversity Management   112

PREFACE

This textbook aims to spice up the classroom experience with engaging mini case studies. Our book is unique in the current market for two reasons. First, it features case studies sufficiently brief that students can reasonably address the issues during a single class period. Some cases are intended to last most of the class period. Others are brief enough to be covered in the last few minutes. Instructors can use these cases to quickly change the pace of classroom dynamics, make a transition between topics, illustrate theoretical concepts, make the most use of all available class time, and encourage active student participation.

Second, although many of these stories have been inspired by real-life experiences to provide an air of authenticity, all of the cases are original fictional narratives. This deliberate fictionalization keeps the cases self-contained, narrows the scope to the issues at hand, and prevents them from being dated too quickly. If your students discover (or think they discover) the real story upon which a case is based, encourage them to use it as a precedent to help them analyze the case at hand. What decisions were made in the real case and what were the consequences? What lessons can be learned that can be applied in the new case? Real public administrators often look to precedents in their own organization's history or from other jurisdictions to guide current decision making.

As instructors, we have polished many of these case studies over time by using them extensively in our classrooms and training workshops. This case-book can serve as a supplementary textbook for general public administration, leadership, human resources management, or administrative ethics courses. To help meet the needs of the instructor, all of the cases are cross-listed among various categories. Discussion questions are included at the end of each case to facilitate thoughtful discussion and analysis.

There are several casebooks on the market, but this book has no equivalent. Case writing in public administration has become intensely sophisticated, often with complex scenarios, richly detailed multi-step simulations, and demanding role-playing requirements. While these types of cases certainly have their place, a less-ambitious style of case writing also has pedagogical value. Short cases provide instructors with maximum flexibility. Students can be required to perform in-depth research on the issues presented within the case prior to class presentation and discussion. Or, the cases can be reviewed rapidly and explored with little preparation. Cases limited to a few facts actually mimic real-life situations in which decision makers must make choices with both incomplete information and time limitations.

For us, a public administrator is someone who works for either a public or nonprofit institution and is at least in charge of a program or supervises other workers. The public inherently invests its administrators with a special trust. The typical public administrator routinely makes decisions that directly or indirectly affect the lives and livelihoods of many others. This book provides an authentic flavor of the work public administrators face. Some challenges are relatively routine while others are much more exciting. Even those situations that on the surface appear mundane often require administrators to make decisions critical for the well-being and livelihood of numerous people. This book reveals that public administrators work in a wide variety of settings. In fact, some people work their entire careers with little recognition that they are in fact public administrators—at least by our definition. University professors are just one example because most (not all) work in either a public or nonprofit institution. We hope that this book tremendously benefits your learning experience.

ACKNOWLEDGMENTS

We would like to thank the peer reviewers who provided valuable feedback throughout the development of this book. They include:

Richard Barton, *George Mason University*
Craig Campbell, *St. Edward's University*
Craig Curtis, *Bradley University*
Sega Howell, *North Carolina Central University*
Scott Moore, *Colorado State University*
Denise Scheberle, *University of Wisconsin—Green Bay*
Robert Schuhmann, *University of Wyoming*
Eric Zeemering, *San Francisco State University*

And those who reviewed anonymously.

ABOUT THE AUTHORS

Brett S. Sharp is a Professor of Political Science and the Director of Leadership Studies at the University of Central Oklahoma. He has published in several scholarly journals including *American Review of Public Administration* and *Review of Public Personnel Administration*. In addition, he has received numerous teaching awards. His previous professional experience includes serving as Employment Manager for the City of Oklahoma City and Agency Services Director for the Oklahoma Office of Personnel Management. He holds a Ph.D. in Political Science and a Master of Public Administration from the University of Oklahoma as well as a B.S. in Political Science with a minor in Religious Studies from Oklahoma State University.

Grant Aguirre is the former General Counsel and Vice President of Human Resources for the American Education Corporation. He is a Lecturer in Political Science, Marketing, and General Business at the University of Central Oklahoma where he also served as the university's Equity Officer. He holds a B.A. and M.A. in Political Science from the University of Central Oklahoma and a J.D. from Oklahoma City University School of Law. In addition, he served as a city council member for the city of Guthrie, Oklahoma. He is now working on his Ph.D. in Marketing from New Mexico State University.

Kenneth Kickham is an Assistant Professor in the Political Science Department at the University of Central Oklahoma. His primary interests are social policy and local government reform. Dr. Kickham's work has appeared in political science and public administration journals including *Public Administration Review* and *Publius*. His previous professional experience includes serving as a comptroller, senior researcher, and management analyst for the Oklahoma Department of Human Services. He is a long-time board member of the National Association for Welfare Research and Statistics. He received his Ph.D. in Political Science and Master of Public Administration from the University of Oklahoma and a B.S. in Accounting from Oklahoma State University.

A Primer on Ethics in Public Administration

WHY STUDY ETHICS?

All of us who have taught ethics for any length of time have had a student who asks the question, "Why should I study ethics in public administration?" As degree programs have become more specialized and technical skills more highly valued, it's a fair question to ask.

The study of philosophical ethics sometimes presents students and practitioners of public administration with more confusion than clarity. What relevance do some ancient Greeks and the more modern ethical thinkers have to today's world? Courses in public finance and accounting, human resources management, public policy implementation, and statistics seem more relevant in the modern world than the obscure and seemingly subjective field of ethics. Finally, many students and practitioners of public administration believe that the law is an adequate minimal standard of behavior, and that if one simply follows the letter of the law, that should be sufficient.

These are fair questions but challenging to answer. We believe that a basic understanding of philosophical ethics is relevant today. There are, quite simply, what we term "perennial issues" that have faced societies from the earliest times. These perennial issues are the questions of knowledge, conduct, and governance. These are the issues that philosophy attempts to answer, and surely these issues are as important for students and practitioners of public administration today as they were for societies throughout history.

Moral philosophy is an activity that allows individuals to think critically about what we can know, how we should act, and what type of governance is best for us. To this end, ethics allows students and practitioners of public administration the opportunity to evaluate competing options and arrive at the best decision.

With regard to the claim that we need to only follow the law, we can say that certainly the law is important, and that the law and ethics are closely related. However, they are not the same. What should we do, for example, if the law is silent on an issue? Or worse yet, what if the law itself is immoral? Again, the study of ethics provides us with a framework to expose these gaps between the law and what is morally right.

Finally, we would point out that public administrators face a host of ethical issues every day, whether they realize it or not. Decisions made by public administrators every day have consequences to the lives of real people. Surely, some understanding of ethics is, therefore, important in dealing with these situations.

Since we have begun by making an argument that the study of ethics is relevant to today's public administrators, we would be remiss if we did not acknowledge and address a number of philosophical challenges to the study of ethics.

SUBJECTIVISM

Subjectivism is the belief that there are no "universal truths." This view can be seen most clearly in the philosophical concept of solipsism. Solipsism is the theory which says that the self is all one can really know.

Subjectivism is attractive because the premise seems to be true. We can never really know what it's like to be someone else, and ethics often seems to be merely a matter of opinion. There don't seem to be "proofs" in ethics the way we have formulas and proofs in science and mathematics. However, we would argue that there are proofs in ethics. One can give good reasons based on rational argumentation for why one choice or solution is better than another. Let's look at an example.

Several years ago, one of us was teaching a course in ethics and had given students their grades on the first essay exam.

After class a student approached the professor and inquired about the grade she had received. She said that she had worked very hard and believed that she deserved a better grade. She followed that observation with the statement, "Look this is all really just your opinion anyway. I have always made A's in high school."

Now, suppose that the professor was unable to articulate any reason for the grade he assigned. If the professor said simply that it was his prerogative to assign grades and could not point to specific reasons, you would surely conclude that the professor's actions were arbitrary, capricious, and not "fair." However, what if the professor could say something like this:

> I asked you to make a decision in this exam based on a set of hypothetical facts. I asked you to make an argument in support of your decision.
> Further, the instructions on the exam stated that you should have a clear and concise thesis statement. And from that thesis statement you should provide substantive premises in support of the thesis in order to reach a logical conclusion. In your paper you told me how you felt, but you failed to support your feelings with a rational set of arguments.

Now further suppose that the professor was accurate in his assessment, and that he was able to provide the student with a model answer that used the method he described above. Would you not say that the professor had acted in a rational and logical manner? Is this not a "proof"? Of course, the student could continue to protest, but such protest would not be rational without any support.

Although proofs in ethics are not as concrete as they are in mathematics, it's important to remember that there are areas of disagreement in the fields of math and science. It's important that we do not employ an incorrect standard. So, we think that we can safely argue that so long as we have an appropriate standard in mind, there are, in fact, proofs in ethics.

CULTURAL RELATIVISM

While subjectivism holds that ethics are based in the individual, cultural relativism holds that ethics are based in the group. That is, what is ethical depends on the culture of a given society. This theory again appears attractive because societies do vary widely in their practice.

For example, the practice of bribing elected officials and public administrators in order to secure government contracts and benefits has long been illegal in the United States. In fact, in response to the "spoils system" of government employment that characterized President Andrew Jackson's administration, the United States has continued to move toward an increasingly professional and technically skilled public workforce. Today, at all levels of government, public administrators are largely selected on the basis of merit rather than political connection.

In many other places in the world, bureaucrats remain grossly underpaid, under-skilled, unprofessional, and corrupt. In many third world and "newly industrialized" nations, the acceptance and expectation of bribery of officials is commonplace. Many executives in multinational corporations argue that such behavior is culturally accepted, and therefore, necessary in order to do business in those countries.

The status of women also differs greatly in different parts of the world. In many places, women are not given the same opportunities that men enjoy in either the public or private sector. Again, many people argue that these differences are cultural and we should respect other people's cultural mores and traditions.

Given our respect for diversity, cultural relativism also seems particularly attractive. Further, it seems that it is supported by the anthropological and sociological record. In fact, we can see evidence of this even in American politics and public administration. Although the United States has certain national cultural values and mores, it also has regional sub-cultural values and mores. State governments differ from each other in many respects. Even rules such as those that prohibit nepotism are subtly different from state to state. In fact, one of the advantages of a federal system of government is that it allows for differences among various regions within a nation.

Although we generally agree that diversity and respect for differing cultures is a good thing, this does not mean that we cannot judge a practice to be unethical. Respect for diversity has its limits when it comes to ethical reasoning.

First, with regard to the subjectivists' claim that there are no universally accepted ideas among various cultures, upon further inspection this claim turns out to be false. It is true that cultures vary widely; however, the claim that there are no a priori universal truths among all societies in the world is categorical. We need only find one exception to this categorical statement and we have disproved the claim. In fact, we can find two prohibitions that apply in all societies. The first is a prohibition against the unjustified killing of a member of one's own group. No society could be formed or sustained that allows the indiscriminate killing of its members by other members. As civilizations have become more advanced, they have extended this protection to individuals from outside the society as well.

The second moral prohibition that can be found even among the most primitive societies is a prohibition against bearing false witness against a member of one's own group. Some level of trust and cooperation is necessary for any society to be sustained. A society that did not have such a prohibition would surely fail as its members would not be able to trust one another and cooperation would be nearly impossible. Again, all modern societies extend this even to individuals from outside the society.

So, we have disproved the claim that there are no "universal truths" that have applied to all societies, but is this all we can say? The answer is no. In fact, if this were all we could say, we would be on very shaky ground. Although we can only identify two "universal truths" that have applied to all societies at all times, we can find many more that have been or are becoming accepted by the vast majority of nations and communities. For example, almost every nation now subscribes (at least in theory) to the ideas that slave labor, unregulated child labor, torture, and genocide are morally reprehensible acts that must not be allowed. The perpetrators committing these acts must be punished.

Further, we must emphasize that there is a difference between what is actually done and how these societies actually feel about such practices. As Socrates points out in *The Republic*, you don't need the philosopher to tell you what is happening, but rather you need the philosopher to tell you what is the best we can become. We believe that although bribery and corruption in the bureaucracies of many countries may occur and even be tolerated, one should not confuse tolerance with moral approval. If one were to ask people in those nations if they approve of such practices, we would speculate that most would answer in the negative. In societies that oppress women, we believe that growing numbers wish it were different.

PSYCHOLOGICAL EGOISM

Psychological egoism is a major challenge to ethics in that it is a deterministic theory. By deterministic, we mean that it posits that people cannot really help the way they act. If this is true, it presents a major problem for ethics because it would be unfair to judge someone for behavior over which he or she has absolutely no control.

Individuals who subscribe to deterministic theories of behavior believe that, either by nature, nurture, or a combination of both, people are programmed and cannot really help but act or react in a given way in any situation. According to this theory, there really is no such thing as free will.

For example, a deterministic argument goes something like this. Suppose that an individual named Smith sees item X. As a result of seeing X, Smith wants X and has the ability to purchase X. However, Smith denies her desire and does not purchase X.

In the above example, most people would argue that it is a clear example of "free will." However, the determinist would argue that it is not "free will" because Smith is not free to want what she wants. Further, her seeming denial of what she wants may be motivated by other desires. She may place a higher value on something else such as the intrinsic satisfaction at showing restraint. However, she is still not free to want that either. Smith may be acting as a result of subconscious factors that even she is not aware of and has no control over.

Psychological egoism is a form of determinism that offers an explanation as to why we behave the way we do. According to this theory, people are inherently selfish. Since we are inherently selfish, psychological egoists argue that we will always act to preserve our own best interests.

At first glance, this theory appears on its face to be false. There are examples of people acting altruistically all the time. Take for example the case of the late Mother Teresa, who spent most of her life caring for the world's poorest, sickest, and most unwanted people. Surely this is a clear example of altruism. The psychological egoist would argue that Mother Teresa was simply doing what she wanted. The psychological egoist would say that she was perhaps motivated by the good feelings that she received as a result of her work, or perhaps by a belief that God told her to do this work and she would not want to disobey God. Whatever the motivation, the psychological egoist would say she was still acting out of a selfish motive.

In response to this descriptive view of human behavior, some thinkers such as Thomas Hobbes have developed a theory called ethical egoism to deal with the problem. According to an ethical egoist, we can channel our selfishness into a positive outcome. This can be seen clearly in Hobbes's statement regarding the state of nature and the subsequent formation of governments to deal with the problems created by the state of nature. Hobbes imagines a time before government when humanity lived in a state that was a "war of all against all" in which life was "solitary, poor, nasty, brutish, and short." However, in this primitive state each individual is absolutely free. Hobbes posits that we came together and formed a "social contract" in which we agreed to give up some of our natural freedoms in exchange for security. In the short term, we may lose something, but it is worth it for the long-term gains that can be achieved in an atmosphere which fosters cooperation. Thus, the major premise is to structure social institutions and rules in such a way as to maximize the overall welfare by using each individual's self-interest.

There are at least three major flaws with psychological egoism. First, it makes a categorical statement about human motivation—that we always act in a selfish manner. In ethics and the social sciences, such categorical statements are usually suspect. People are enormously complex and it is impossible to say what has and continues to motivate every person since the beginning of mankind. Also, the theory does not adequately address the fact that people are often enormously conflicted about the choices they make.

A second problem with the theory is that it treats selfishness and self-interest as synonyms. These terms are not one and the same. Getting a college education is surely in one's self-interest, but it is not selfish. In fact, one could argue that getting an education is the antithesis of being selfish. Statistically we know that people with more education are likely to be more self-sufficient at least in economic terms. Therefore, an individual with more education is less likely to be a burden on his or her family or society, and this is the opposite of being selfish.

Finally, psychological egoism equates motives with feelings. For example, suppose that Smith helps Jones make some repairs to his home because she cannot afford to hire someone. Smith may feel good about having helped Jones, but that's not necessarily her motivation.

Now that we have addressed three of the most serious challenges to ethical reasoning, let us now turn to the major ethical theories. Each of these theories has its advantages and disadvantages. We will conclude this section with what we believe is an acceptable "moral minimum."

UTILITARIAN THEORY (TELEOLOGICAL ETHICS)

This theory was largely developed by late 18th and early 19th century thinkers such as Jeremy Bentham and John Stuart Mill. This theory holds that acts are judged to be morally right or wrong not in and of themselves, but rather by the *results* that follow from the acts. Therefore, no act is in and of itself right or wrong.

For example, according to this theory, lying is not always morally reprehensible. If good results follow from lying, then the lie is justified. On the other hand, if a lie leads to bad results, then it is morally wrong. In his *Utilitarianism*, Mill stated:

> The creed which accepts as the foundation of morals, utility, or the greatest happiness principle, holds that actions are right in proportion as they tend to promote happiness, wrong as they tend to produce the reverse of happiness. By happiness is intended pleasure, and the absence of pain; by unhappiness, pain and the privation of pleasure. To give a clear view of the moral standard set up by the theory, much more requires to be said; in particular what things it includes in the ideas of pain and pleasure; and to what extent this is left an open question. But these supplementary explanations do not affect the theory of life on which this theory of morality is grounded–namely, that pleasure, and freedom from pain, are the only things desirable as ends; and that all

desirable things (which are as numerous in the utilitarian as in any other scheme) are desirable either for the pleasure inherent in themselves, or as means to the promotion of pleasure and the prevention of pain.

Let us examine how this theory works in a modern bureaucracy. The example we will employ will be a police department. We will use an example from what economists call game theory, and the "prisoner's dilemma" specifically.

Suppose that two individuals commit a crime together and subsequently get caught. After arresting them the police will want to question these individuals; however, they will not do so with them present in each other's company. The officers will place the individuals in two separate interrogation rooms. Now further suppose that the police do not have enough evidence to convict either of the individuals of the crime for which they are accused unless one or both of them makes a confession. If neither individual talks they can get a conviction on a lesser offense. If one individual talks and his or her fellow prisoner does not, the one that talks will receive a lighter sentence. However, if both prisoners talk, they will receive the maximum sentence under the law. Now, further suppose that both prisoners are aware of all the choices and consequences, but neither is aware of what the other inmate is doing. This is called a game of complete but imperfect knowledge. The game is complete because each prisoner knows all the possible choices and outcomes, but it is imperfect because he or she does not know how the other prisoner will behave or is behaving.

The police in this case will exploit the imperfect knowledge aspect of the situation by engaging in lying. An interrogating officer may say to one of the prisoners, "Your fellow prisoner is about to break. So, you might as well tell us the truth, and things will go a lot easier on you." In all likelihood another officer is saying the same thing to the second prisoner. The end result is that in most cases as a result of the deception by the police both prisoners end up talking, and each is worse off than he or she would have been had he or she maintained his or her constitutional right to remain silent.

		P_1	
		Talk	Remain Silent
P_2	Talk	10, 10	10, 7
	Remain Silent	7, 10	3, 3
		(Payoffs P_1, P_2)	

EXHIBIT 1.1

Prisoners Dilemma

From a utilitarian perspective, lying in this case might be justified. Two individuals who have committed a crime will be put in jail, and society will be protected. Thus by lying, the officer has promoted the greatest good for the most number of people, that is society as a whole, since a crime is technically a breach of a duty we owe to society as a whole.

On the other hand, it probably would not be morally acceptable, from a utilitarian perspective, for citizens to lie to the police. Lying to the police could lead to a waste of time and resources and criminals might actually get away with crime. This would lead to less happiness and therefore would be ethically wrong.

Students often like this theory because it does seem to be the way in which we normally make judgments. It seems almost intuitive. In fact, this theory has had a great impact on the economic system of the United States. More than other Western nations, Americans believe in the free hand of the market which is predicated on utilitarian grounds, that is the maximization of utility.

Utilitarianism, however, does have a number of problems. First, there are some things that most of us just believe are a priori wrong even if they do bring about good results. For example, let us suppose that a police officer has just apprehended a serial killer. The officer knows beyond any doubt that the killer is in fact guilty. However, the officer knows that if the killer goes to trial, the evidence against him is largely circumstantial, and he or she may be acquitted. Further, the officer knows that he or she will be appointed counsel, as required by the Sixth Amendment, at great expense to the state. The state will also incur great expenses in terms of having to produce its expert witnesses. Valuable court time will be spent, wasting even more resources. Then even if a conviction is obtained, the officer knows that this individual will most likely file appeals all of which will be paid for by the state. Therefore, the officer makes the decision to shoot the killer, and make it look like he was defending himself. If all of the facts in this hypothetical are true, based on utilitarian principles, the officer would be morally justified in his or her action. However, most of us believe that this would be morally reprehensible. The United States prides itself on being a nation of laws, not of men. In this case, the officer has taken the law into his or her own hands. He or she has acted as investigator, judge, jury, and executioner. In this case, very few people would be willing to say that the officer acted in an ethical manner.

One could argue that our entire legal system with its allowance of multiple appeals is cumbersome and inefficient. In spite of this, most of us are not willing to change it for a more utilitarian one. Many of us still believe that we would rather see many guilty people go free than one innocent person executed.

In order to address the problems associated with this first challenge to utilitarianism, some ethicists have developed a modified version of utilitarianism called "rule utilitarianism." The original version of utilitarianism might be called "act utilitarianism" in that it formulated a method for dealing with discrete situations. Those who subscribe to act utilitarianism usually view each situation as unique. No two situations are ever completely identical. Therefore, in each situation, the actor must analyze the situation, develop possible solutions, and chose the solution that will promote the greatest good or happiness.

Although it is true that no two situations are completely identical, the range of human experience is such that certain commonalities or patterns can be discerned. Ethicists who subscribe to rule utilitarianism believe that we can develop rules from these commonalities that over time will produce the greatest happiness. The objective for the rule utilitarian is to discern rules that may not in any particular instance lead to the greatest happiness at the time, but will over the long haul produce the best results.

Returning to our example of the officer and the serial killer above, the rule utilitarian would say the officer did not act ethically because he or she violated a rule that was ultimately intended to produce the greatest happiness. A rule utilitarian would argue that although in this instance if the officer failed to kill the criminal it would lead to less utility, that nonetheless he or she should refrain from committing the act. Although our legal system is slow and costly, one should not assume too quickly that it does not produce the greatest happiness. For example, if people believed that officers often took the law into their own hands and dispensed vigilante justice, they would rightly be suspicious of the police. Such suspicion would lead people to be hesitant to aid the police. The lack of trust and subsequent aid would ultimately lead to terrible results. However, because we believe in the rule of law in this country and most believe that generally the police follow the rule of law, most people cooperate with law enforcement.

There is a second challenge to utilitarianism and this one may be even more relevant to students of public administration. The examples presented above are fairly straightforward because we have made a number of suppositions. In the real world, things are rarely as cut and dry. Most situations are extremely complex and it may be impossible to foresee the outcome of a given situation with any degree of certainty. Highly complex decisions often result in unintended side effects or what economists term, "externalities."

The problem of externalities is highlighted by the analogy of the "tragedy of the commons." Suppose that public land owned by the government is made available for the grazing of herd animals such as sheep. This land is what is called a "public good" because anyone can enjoy its use. "Private goods" on the other hand are ones that are owned by individuals who can exclude others from using them. For example, Smith owns a tract of land. Smith can stop others from trespassing on her land and using it. The public land that is made available for the grazing of sheep is likely to become overused because it does not cost the sheep herders anything to use. Therefore, each sheep herder has an incentive to graze as many sheep as he or she wants. The end result is destruction of the public land such that no one is able to benefit from the "public good." The private land owner on the other hand is less likely to misuse her land by overgrazing because she has an investment in the land. If she destroys her land, she will ultimately pay the price for the destruction.

The Environmental Protection Agency is a modern bureaucracy that was created as a result of such externalities. During the latter half of the nineteenth century and early part of the twentieth century, our nation experienced rapid industrialization. Many at the time believed that this was a good thing, and in many respects it was. However, our lack of understanding of the effects on the environment at the time has led to some serious consequences that current and future generations now have to address. During the early years of industrialization, no one knew what disastrous effects pollution would have, not only on our environment but on our own health as well. As a result of pollution, we have seen increases in things like respiratory and allergy problems. Hindsight is always 20/20. Would it be fair to judge the great industrialists of the nineteenth century as immoral for consequences they could not have known about?

Although utilitarianism does have a number of problems, this ethical theory does provide us with at least one useful analytical tool. Utilitarianism forces us to consider alternatives and to use logic in the consideration of possible alternatives.

DUTY ETHICS (DEONTOLOGICAL ETHICS)

In contrast to teleological ethics above, deontological or duty ethics is not concerned with the consequences of an act. Duty ethics says that we are morally obligated to act in a certain way regardless of consequence. Thus, those that ascribe to this theory deny that "the ends justify the means."

In order to begin to understand the difference between teleological ethics and deontological ethics, let us look at a modern example that has made headlines in recent times. The example we shall use is child labor. In our modern American society, child labor is highly regulated by both the United States Department of Labor and the various state departments of labor. Children in the United States are permitted to work. But the jobs they are allowed to perform are limited by the Fair Labor Standards Act of 1938 (FLSA) and by various state labor laws. With regard to children, the FLSA's purpose is to protect their educational opportunities and prohibit their employment in jobs that are detrimental to their safety or health. For example, under Title 29 of the United States Code of Federal Regulations, children 15 years of age and younger are prohibited from working in "manufacturing, mining, or processing occupations, including occupations requiring the performance of any duties in work rooms or work places where goods are manufactured, mined, or otherwise processed . . ." (29 CFR 570.33). The United States regulation of child labor was a response to the exploitation of child labor during the early part of the industrial revolution when children from poor families were employed in dangerous industries. Today, we recognize that education of our children is necessary and that they should not be permitted to work in facilities that interfere with their education or present a hazard to their safety and health.

As the industrialized nations of the world began to eliminate child labor in manufacturing and other dangerous occupations, many of these manufacturing and dangerous jobs have been moved to lesser developed nations where child labor laws are either nonexistent or unenforced. U.S. businesses such as Nike,

Wal-Mart, The Gap, Levi Strauss, Target, Donna Karan, New Balance, Disney, Reebok, Adidas, Van Heusen, Liz Claiborne, Ralph Lauren, and Kathie Lee Gifford were using manufacturers in third-world nations to produce their goods. These manufacturers employed sweatshop conditions and exploited child labor.

Many economists and utilitarian ethicists argue that this is part of development and not necessarily a bad thing. From a utilitarian perspective, overall happiness is achieved by such practices. People in the United States and other industrialized nations get goods at a cheap cost, while those in the developing world benefit from making wages necessary to support themselves and their families. As those nations continue to develop and as technology continues to advance, child labor in those places will also end just as it has in the United States. However, at this time, sweatshop conditions and child labor are the reality. Many individuals from the developing world point out that our own past gives us little room to criticize. Therefore, utilitarian ethicists justify such practices based on a cost/benefit analysis.

For a duty ethicist, sweatshops and unregulated child labor are deplorable, inhumane, and unethical practices. Taking advantage of people who have little or no choice violates the autonomy of those that are exploited and our own humanity. No amount of economic utility can be used to justify such practices. For those that ascribe to deontological ethics, the use of child labor in sweatshops is a priori wrong. The fact that we in the United States at one time permitted such conditions to exist is beside the point and not a defense. Deontological ethicists would say that we have a duty to not engage in such methods and that those in the United States that employed them in the past were also guilty of a grave moral wrong. As to the argument that this is "just the way things are," a duty ethicist would again point out that it is not the business of philosophy to tell us what has occurred or is occurring, but rather it is the business of philosophy to discover what is best.

Naturally, deontological ethics raises the question of what constitutes a duty. In other words, assuming that we do have "duties," what are they and how can we know them? The German philosopher Immanuel Kant provided a method by which we can discern what our duties are in his *Foundations of the Metaphysics of Morals* (1785).

Kant distinguished between two types of imperatives: hypothetical and categorical. Hypothetical imperatives are a result of some desire. For example, we know that people with college degrees typically earn more money than people who only possess a high school diploma. Therefore, if you want a better chance of earning a higher income, you should go to college. In many instances, these types of imperatives are amoral, but not necessarily so. For some people, earning a high income or having what society perceives as a prestigious job is simply not important and there is no moral import to that. Of course, some desires may have moral import such as obtaining something by stealing. The important point here is that hypothetical imperatives exist because we have some desire.

On the other hand, Kant says that categorical imperatives exist because man is the rational animal. According to Kant, we can determine moral imperatives using the following formulation: Act only according to the maxim by which you can at the same time will that it should become a universal law.

For Kant, we should in all other actions with rational beings (i.e., other people) treat people as an end and not as a means to an end. This means that when faced with a moral dilemma, we must formulate a rule that is logically consistent at all times, and then we must be willing to act on that logic. For example, lying is never permissible according to Kant. He would not permit lying even for altruistic motives.

There are a couple of problems with Kant's categorical imperative. First, it allows for no exceptions. However, for almost every rule there are exceptions. Of course, the exceptions should be rare, but nonetheless they exist. Let us take a look at an example; the case is called the hypothetical of the inquiring murderer. Suppose that an abused wife whose husband has threatened to kill her if she leaves confides in you that she is leaving her husband, and she is going to hide out at the local shelter for abused women. Now, further suppose the husband asks you where his wife is, and states that he believes that she may be at the local shelter. You reasonably know that if you don't tell the husband a lie he will likely find the wife and kill her. Kant would say that you have to tell the truth. However, this seems too harsh for most people. The reason that Kant would say that you have to tell the truth is because lying can't be a universal law. However, it seems to us that the reason that this cannot be a universal law is because if people lied all the time, no one would trust anyone else and ultimately it would be hard to form any type of society. But isn't this really another way of saying that ultimately consequences really do matter?

Another problem with Kant's formulation is that rules often conflict. We are left with little guidance as to what we should do when the rules contradict each other. Let us return to the case of the inquiring murderer above. It is perfectly logically consistent to have a rule that says that you shouldn't participate in the killing of an innocent person. However, in the case above you are left with two choices. You tell the husband the truth and he kills his wife, making you a participant in her death, or you lie to him saving the wife, but committing the moral wrong of lying.

Despite its problems, Kant's categorical imperative is useful for a couple of reasons. First, Kant forces us to be rational. Kant's insistence on logic forces us to consider our actions in the cold light of reason. If you accept that morality must be based on rationality, then it must be rational at all the times. You cannot accept rationality in one instance and not another. A second advantage of Kant's philosophy is that it forces the individual to admit that he or she is subject to the same moral imperatives as everyone else. No one can claim to be "special," and therefore, exempt from morality.

VIRTUE ETHICS

Virtue ethics can be traced back to Aristotle and his two major ethical works *Nichomachean Ethics* and *Eudemain Ethics*. The idea behind virtue ethics is that we should determine what characteristics are desirable and then try to promote those characteristics in people.

In order to determine what types of characteristics we should promote, it is necessary to determine what type of being we are. In other words, Aristotle asks what the "end" of a human being is. What is it we are made to do? In many translations of Aristotle, he says that the purpose of a human being is "happiness." We, however, agree with Professor Daniel Robinson that happiness (as in "drink-up let's have another round") is a limited concept, and therefore, a more appropriate concept would be that the end of a human being is a flourishing life.

In order to achieve the flourishing life, Aristotle thought one should habitually engage in practicing the virtues. Aristotle said that the virtues were derived from the mean between two extremes. For example, cowardice is an extreme defect of character. The opposite of cowardice is heedlessness. The mean between these two extremes is courage. The coward is one who always runs away from any confrontation. The heedless person is willing to fight at the slightest provocation, but the courageous person knows when to "fight the good fight." Some of the other virtues would include: generosity, patience, tactfulness, tolerance, loyalty, civility, and compassion to name just a few.

The critics of Aristotle's virtue ethics question how we can know what the end of a human being is. Who is to say that happiness or a flourishing life is the purpose of a human being? Religious absolutists of many varieties would say that the worship and acceptance of the laws of a given deity are the reason we exist.

A second criticism of virtue ethics is what makes these virtues the right ones. One might argue that moderation in the face of vice is no virtue at all. For example, many people believe that indulgence in any kind of alcohol or drug is wrong, and therefore, no amount of moderation is acceptable.

A final criticism is that it is not clear that even if we agree on some purpose of a human life, and then agree on what constitutes virtues, that these can be taught. For example, there are many examples throughout history of governments and the people who work for them engaging in cruelty of the most vicious sort. Nazi Germany is but one example; however, such examples are not, unfortunately, relegated to any one period or even the past. Do we really think that we could have reformed a Hitler, Stalin, or Saddam Hussein?

In spite of the criticism, virtue ethics is something we should seriously consider because it does offer a holistic approach. Also, we can think of at least one notable example in which it does seem to have worked. One of America's founding fathers, Benjamin Franklin, noticed at an early age that he had certain leadership qualities. He also noticed that he engaged in some behaviors that people didn't like. As a young man, he was fond of making up puns, and he noticed that people thought of him as a jokester. Franklin set about reforming himself and came up with a list of virtues that he tried to practice every day. From all outward appearances, Franklin's personal psychological experiment seems to have worked. Franklin rose from modest beginnings to become a successful man, politician, diplomat, writer, and inventor.

THE MORAL MINIMUM

Now that we have presented most of the major ethical theories along with their shortcomings, students often ask us what a moral minimum standard would entail. Based on our study of ethics we believe that a moral minimum would consist of a number of components. However, we must caution that any such list of components is just a minimum. We believe that an acceptable moral minimum would entail the following:

1. When faced with an ethical dilemma you must, to the extent possible, be objective.
2. You must be willing to analyze the situation and develop possible solutions, and you must be willing to consider other people's ideas if they are presented.
3. You must be willing to consider the impact your decision will have on all parties involved.
4. Your decision should be based on a logical analysis of your known possible solutions.
5. Finally, you must be willing to act on this rational analysis.

THE CASE STUDY METHOD

Now that we have provided you with an overview of the major ethical theories, for the remainder of the text we have provided fact patterns that present a variety of managerial and ethical issues in public administration. The discussion questions ask you to analyze these case studies from a variety of perspectives and, using the various ethical theories, determine what you think is the best possible solution to the situation.

In thinking about these cases and the ethical theories, we believe that a useful method is the IRAC method. IRAC stands for issue, rule, application, and conclusion.

First, as you read the cases, you should identify all the issues involved. Some of the cases present only one or two issues, while others are more complex and present multiple issues that you should identify.

Second, based on the ethical theories, what rules or principles would apply to the situation? You should think about each theory.

The third step is the application. How would the rules/principles of each theory apply to the fact pattern presented?

Finally, you should reach a conclusion. You should think about the conclusion that would be reached by a theorist from each of the major theories, and then develop the conclusion that you think is the best.

Managing Employees

CASE 1: FLOGGINGS WILL CONTINUE

For the very first time in the history of the State Department of Environmental Quality (DEQ), a governor was taking the time to visit the agency. The DEQ Director escorted the governor and a small entourage. They walked around the offices and the governor visited with various state employees. He went to the basement and visited workers in the Air Quality Control Division. As he went inside one office to shake an inspector's hand, he saw a cartoon on the worker's bulletin board. It looked like an old-fashioned woodprint illustrating sailors and naval officers on the deck of a wooden sailing ship. In the picture, the master-at-arms stood stiffly by as the chief boatswain's mate took a cat o' nine tails (basically, nine small leather whips attached to a wooden baton) across the bare back of an errant sailor. The caption below the picture read in big letters, "The Floggings Will Continue Until Morale Improves."

The governor stopped and stiffened. Then he asked the worker, "Do you really feel this way?"

"It's just a joke . . . it's just meant to be funny."

"What's your name?"

"I'm Dan . . . uh, . . . Daniel. Daniel Welles."

"Dan, if you have any concerns that you think should come to my attention, give me a call directly." The governor wrote a number on a sticky pad and handed it to Dan. The governor then left to visit the rest of the agency.

The DEQ Director motioned Dan's supervisor to come forward and he whispered in her ear, "I want you to terminate Daniel's employment by the end of this week. That was embarrassing. Do whatever you need to do."

DISCUSSION QUESTIONS

1. Is the governor's style of leadership—walking around and talking directly with frontline workers—admirable? What are the advantages and disadvantages of this strategy?
2. Did the governor cross a line by talking directly with a state employee and not going through the normal chain of command?

3. Has the DEQ Director overreacted? If so, what option does Dan's supervisor have, if any?
4. If you were Dan's supervisor, would you terminate Dan's employment? Why or why not? If terminated, what actions should Dan take?

CASE 2: NOT PAYING TAXES AT THE IRS

The Commissioner of the Internal Revenue Service (IRS) discovered that a number of the agency's employees were years behind in filing their federal income tax returns. The Commissioner believed this represented a serious breach of ethical conduct. After all, these employees worked for the very agency responsible for enforcement of the federal tax code and taxpayer filings. In reality, the vast majority of the employees who failed to file their returns were owed a refund. However, the Commissioner issued an internal policy memo that stated:

> A significant number of IRS employees are one or more years behind in filing their personal income tax returns. The IRS is the agency charged with the duty to enforce our nation's tax code. As such, employees of this agency should be beyond reproach with regard to the filing of their own personal federal income tax returns. The failure of any employee of this agency to file his or her personal income tax return represents a serious lapse of the employee's ethical duty to this agency and the taxpayers we serve.
>
> I have directed the Office of Human Resources to develop a policy for the employee policy manual that states that employees who are two or more years behind in the filing of their personal federal income tax returns may be subject to disciplinary action up to and including immediate termination.

In response to the Commissioner's memo, the Office of Human Resources promulgated a policy that IRS employees were expected, as a condition of employment, to promptly file their personal income tax returns. The policy went on to make clear that unless an employee suffered an "extreme hardship," failure to file personal income taxes for two or more consecutive years could lead to disciplinary action, including termination. The agency provided that any employee who was delinquent as of the date of the policy's adoption would be given a six-month grace period, starting from the date of its publication in the updated employee policy manual, to come into compliance with the policy. The policy was adopted on March 1, 2003 and an e-mail regarding the policy was sent to all employees of the agency. An updated employee policy manual which contained the new policy was printed and distributed to all employees on July 1, 2003. Thus employees were sent two notices regarding the new policy, giving them until January 1, 2004 to come into compliance.

June Adkins was a Senior Internal Revenue Agent who had been employed for over twenty years with the agency since having graduated with a Master of Science in Accountancy and passing her CPA exam on the first try.

June was in all respects a model employee. She had always received the highest evaluations on her performance appraisals and had additionally received numerous service awards during her tenure. Although citizens whose finances are audited by the IRS are generally resentful, June had a way of making most people feel at ease. Her supervisor often received letters praising June's handling of particular cases.

Beginning in 2001, June experienced a number of personal difficulties beginning with her father's diagnosis of lung cancer. During the year, June's parents relied on her to help with the treatment regimen her father was undergoing. When her father died, June's mother turned to her to help probate the estate and file the necessary state and federal tax returns. June was appointed the personal representative of her father's estate and had to spend a great deal of her personal time settling the estate.

The following year, June and her husband began to experience marital difficulties in their ten-year marriage. The marriage ultimately ended in a bitter divorce and the property settlement battle continued through most of 2003 until a decree of divorce was finally granted on December 19, 2003.

Through all her personal problems, June continued to work as a model employee, fulfilling the specific job functions of her position. Although she received both the e-mail and new employee policy manual, she failed to notice them.

Due to her personal problems, June did not file income tax returns for 2001, 2002, or 2003 on time. Kevin Lair, June's supervisor, was made aware of her delinquency after the April 15, 2004 deadline for filing of 2003 taxes.

On her W-4 form, June claimed zero dependants even though she could claim at least herself and her husband. Based on her familiarity with the tax code she knew that she was owed a refund for all three years.

In early May, Kevin approached June and said, "June, there is a matter of some urgency that I need to discuss with you. Would you please meet with me in my office this afternoon at 3:00?"

"Sure, Kevin," June replied. June just assumed that the meeting was regarding one of her ongoing audits. That afternoon, June was shocked when she walked into the meeting and a member of the human resources team was there.

Kevin began by saying, "June, I am sure you know that a policy memo went out from the Commissioner in 2003 stating that the agency was aware that a significant number of its employees were behind in the filing of their personal income tax returns."

"Well, no Kevin, I actually don't remember that memo," June replied.

"Are you saying that you don't read the memos that the Commissioner puts out?"

"No, Kevin, I do read the memos that the Commissioner puts out. What I am saying is that I don't recall that specific memo."

"Well, what about a subsequent e-mail sent on March 1, 2003 from human resources that was sent to all employees notifying them of the new policy established in response to the Commissioner's memo, do you remember that?"

"No, Kevin I don't remember that either," said June.

"Well, following the memo a new employee policy manual was sent to all employees, do you remember that?" Kevin asked.

"I do remember getting my new policy manual. I skimmed it to see if there were any major changes to it since the last edition, and I didn't remember seeing anything significant."

"So, what you are saying is that you don't read any of the changes in policies and procedures that affect your job here at the IRS?" Kevin asked.

"That is absolutely not what I am saying, Kevin! I do read those things. I am just saying that I don't know or can't remember if I read the specific policy you are talking about."

"Under the policy, we are supposed to terminate an employee who is more than two years behind on filing income taxes, June," said Kevin.

"Kevin, I can't believe this is happening to me. I have been a good employee. In 2001, my father was diagnosed with cancer and I had to help take care of him. He died later that year and I had to probate his estate and file his estate tax returns. Then my marriage of ten years fell apart. I was dealing with a messy divorce and a husband who was trying to claim all of the deductions during the time we were married. I was fighting him in court on a number of issues. Honestly, it is not that I have intentionally not filed. I knew that I was owed a refund for all three years based on my allowable deductions and number of dependants I claimed on my W-4 form."

"Well, June, I don't know that I have a lot of choice in this matter. I will have to talk to my boss about this situation. We are meeting this afternoon and I know this topic will come up, and I'll have to get back with you after that," replied Kevin.

DISCUSSION QUESTIONS

1. In theory, is the new policy a good idea? Why or why not? Should the policy be rewritten to provide more clarification? Is it too draconian as written? What ethical theory or theories would support the new policy?
2. Does June's situation qualify for a hardship exemption from the policy? What about her claim that she does not remember any of the communications regarding the policy? There were three communications sent out about the policy. Shouldn't a diligent employee have read at least one of those communications?
3. How would you evaluate Kevin's actions in this case? Could he have taken a different approach? Was it necessary to get human resources involved before he knew all the facts? Was Kevin's statement of the policy accurate? Was this statement ethical? Should he have provided a copy of the actual policy to June for her review? Why or why not?
4. If a decision is made to terminate an employee under this or any other policy of a government agency, how much due process should be afforded an employee to ensure that a wrongful termination does not occur, or that if one should occur, the employee is reinstated? What would you say is the essence of the concept of "due process?"

CASE 3: CUTTING LOOSE THE DIRTY DOZEN

"The reason why I have gathered you here this morning and invited your union representatives is that I am going to make an announcement. I wanted you to hear it from me first, before it's made public." Marisa Munson paused and then took a sip of water from the bottle she was holding in her hand. She knew this would be difficult news for these twelve employees, but as the Director of Water Utilities for the city, she felt it was her duty. "As of July 1, the start of the new fiscal year, we are contracting out the services of this Wastewater Inspection Division to WMG Services. This action is not being taken without great thought and analysis. The fact is that WMG Services will be able to deliver more coverage and higher quality lab analysis using the most up-to-date technologies. They can do this at a fraction of the cost of retaining this function ourselves. With me today are some folks from the city's human resources management office. They will explain the layoff procedures and how it will impact you personally. But before I turn it over to them, my staff and I are available to answer any questions you may have."

The first one up was the union president who asked, "Why weren't we consulted about this? According to contract, you are to give us timely notice of any layoffs."

"This is your timely notice," explained Marisa. "Your members have almost three months before this takes effect to make the appropriate preparations."

"We don't have to take this!" And with that the union president and his assistant stomped out of the room. The twelve wastewater employees looked as if they were in shock. No one asked any questions. Marisa then turned over the meeting to the personnel staff who began speaking to each of the wastewater employees individually.

As Marisa and her staff started to leave the room, Employment Manager Richard Box motioned Marisa over to him. He whispered, "Marisa, your decision is going against our recommendations. You and I both know that you're not doing this because you think that the duties of the Wastewater Inspection Division would be handled better by a private vendor. You're doing this because you're tired of dealing with the turmoil this division has caused over the past several months."

"I'm sure I don't know what you mean."

"Don't play coy. I've heard you call them the 'dirty dozen' because they are always filing grievances against each other and their supervisors. You asked me the other day how you should handle the fact that this entire division is not covering its responsibilities. I told you to use the performance appraisal and progressive discipline systems. You complained about their lack of work performance, but when I checked their evaluations, you and your supervisors in the field had given them fairly high marks." Richard stopped to take a breath. "Now you may have solved *your* problem, but you've caused more work for me. In the end you won't help the city at all. My staff is damn good at placing employees in these reduction-in-force situations into other vacant city positions. With the good performance evaluations of these employees, they will stay with the city. You're not solving anything—you're just shoving your problem off on other departments."

"Think what you like, but I believe this is in the best interests of the city. WMG Services has been a proven partner for this department and they certainly came through last summer when the dry spell put such a strain on our aging water system. Plus we get access to the latest technologies with no up-front capital expenditures on our part."

Before she left, Marisa turned to Richard again, winked, and then said very quietly, "Another side benefit of my decision is that every employee in every other unit in our department will get the clear message to focus on their jobs and *not* spend time making trouble for the rest of us."

DISCUSSION QUESTIONS

1. Were the union leaders justified in leaving the meeting in such an abrupt manner? Does such a dramatic but short-lived protest over a decision that has already been made outweigh possible concessions union leaders might gain by learning more about the decision and continuing the dialogue with management? In your opinion, have the union employees been well represented?
2. Should Richard take his concerns about Marisa's true motives up the chain of command? How should Marisa's supervisor respond if presented with Richard's concerns?
3. Given the legal and procedural constraints placed on public managers, is Marisa justified in using every means at her disposal to make her department more productive? Should a manager give priority to the needs of his or her department over the larger organization?
4. When making a decision concerning the overall structure of an organization, is it a good management practice to take into account the performance of individual employees? Or should those considerations be handled by the performance appraisal process?

CASE 4: ELEVEN MONTHS TO RETIREMENT

On his sixty-fourth birthday, Mani Swaminathan, a prized and well-respected employee, visited the agency's benefits representative to make preparations for his retirement.

Mani had been born and raised in Sri Lanka but had left for England as a young man and had worked in the British civil service. Then, after immigrating to the United States, he had become an American citizen and for the past twenty years had worked in state government. Now he wanted to retire while he was still young enough to visit his family, which by this time had settled all over the world. In particular, he wanted to spend some time with his grandchildren living in India. He decided he would retire within the year.

Mani informed his supervisor, Will Fairchild, who responded, "I mean it when I say you have been my most valued worker and we will miss you greatly.

I'll do my best to make sure that your last months here are pleasant. If there is any project you feel particularly enthusiastic about completing before you go, I'll try my best to allow you the time to do it."

A couple of weeks passed, and Carli Buster approached Will with a concern. "Since you're my supervisor as well as Mani's, I need you to know that I am doing almost all of his work now. He spends the early part of his mornings walking around the building talking with people. At mid-morning he disappears and returns early afternoon as if he had taken a long lunch. And then he usually leaves well before the official end of the workday. The only time I see him is when he drops by my office to talk. And he almost always leaves one of his assignments for me to complete."

Will looked surprised and responded, "I didn't realize it was that bad. I think Mani is just tired and burned out and he's got a short-timer's attitude. I honestly didn't think he would ever want to retire, but that seems to be all he's living for now. You know, I could come down hard on him and make him really produce, but he's only got eleven months to go and I just don't have the heart to keep the pressure on him. Before I was his supervisor, he was mine. Mani was good to me. He was my mentor. He's always worked harder than anybody else and he's always been supportive of all of his colleagues. If you don't mind, I'm going to let him spend his remaining days with us in peace. I'll keep in mind that you're now working extra hard and I'll find some way to make it worth your while."

DISCUSSION QUESTIONS

1. How much consideration should a supervisor give to an employee such as Mani who has been a star performer for years, but then begins to coast as well-earned retirement approaches?
2. Should Will place a little extra pressure on Mani to boost his performance for the next several months? Why or why not?
3. How should Carli respond to Will's decision to maintain the status quo? Should she continue to take up the slack for Mani? Would it be appropriate for Carli to go up the chain of command with her concerns? Explain your answer.
4. Will makes an indefinite promise to Carli to reward her for her extra work. Assume that an opportunity for promotion becomes available in the next several months for employees under Will's supervision. Should he give Carli any kind of edge in the competitive promotion process? What weight should he give to the merit of other employees?

CASE 5: A COMPETENT BUT SLOW EMPLOYEE

First Deputy County Clerk Christie Baird was reviewing the personnel file of Heather Points, an employee she had hired almost six months earlier. Heather had been hired to replace a young woman named Rebecca Luker who had left the Clerk's Office to go back to college and finish her degree. Rebecca had been a model employee. She had been easy to get along with, and everyone in the office had really liked her.

In addition to her outgoing personality, Rebecca had a good work ethic and she had quickly learned all the computer programs in the office as well as the land records which were kept in both electronic and hard copy formats as required by state law.

When Rebecca left, everyone knew that she would be hard to replace and that anyone who did take her place would have "big shoes to fill." Heather was chosen from a candidate pool of twenty-four applicants most of whom were at least partially qualified for the position as it was advertised. Heather was forty-nine when she was hired, and although she had a different personality than Rebecca, most people in the office felt she would be the best fit for the position. They thought that, due to her age, Heather would be less likely than younger candidates to leave after only a year or two to return to school. In addition, Heather had worked in a law office as a legal secretary in her last position. Most people in the office thought her experience would be beneficial to the Clerk's Office. Most importantly, the hiring committee was enthused about Heather's pleasing personality and, as a result, did not feel the need to conduct as thorough a reference check as they would normally.

After six months, Christie was beginning to have doubts about Heather. Heather had been slow to learn how the state indexed land records; after two rounds of training she was now only minimally competent. She was still struggling with the indexing methodology. Christie inquired about Heather's previous job, "I thought that you worked in a law office prior to working here. Didn't you already have experience with land and title records, indexes, and searches?" Heather explained that she had worked for a firm that handled personal injury cases only and that she had no experience in real property law as a result.

In addition to having trouble with the land records, Heather struggled to learn the computer programs in the office. After nearly six months, Heather was minimally competent in all of her duties, and many of the functions of the office had slowed down since Rebecca left. Since the Clerk's Office was already operating on an almost "skeleton staff," every individual in the office had to interact and rely on every other staff member. As a result, Christie was seriously considering recommending that the County Clerk Kelly Monden terminate Heather's employment prior to the end of her probationary period while she could still be let go without cause. After the probationary period, the policy of the County Board of Commissioners was that an employee could only be fired for "just and good cause." Christie's only hesitation was that it would take some time to train a new employee and get them up to speed.

DISCUSSION QUESTIONS

1. If you were in Christie's position, what would you do and why?
2. Is it ethical to fire a "minimally competent" employee before their probationary period ends simply because they are only "minimally competent." What ethical theory can be used to justify such a decision?

3. Do you think that Heather is being unfairly compared to her predecessor? If she is being compared to Rebecca, is that ethical? Does the fact that the Clerk's Office is operating on a "skeleton staff" make any difference in your answer? Should it?

4. Was it ethical for members of the staff to consider Heather's age in the hiring process? In this case, the fact that Heather was older actually worked to her advantage; however, in many cases age is a disadvantage. What arguments can be made that age is a relevant factor? What arguments can be made that it's not? Does it depend on the position? What about the Age Discrimination in Employment Act (ADEA)—does the existence of a law prohibiting age discrimination change your answer? How important a consideration is "personality" when making a new hire?

CASE 6: A TERMINATION BY ANY OTHER NAME

Jeffrey Deck, Assistant Federal Security Director for the Transportation Security Administration (TSA) at the Raleigh-Durham Airport in North Carolina, was hearing those familiar words in his head over and over. "No good deed goes unpunished," his wife Elaine had warned. It seemed she was right. As Jeffrey walked down the hallway to a meeting with Renaldo Wong, TSA's Southeast Area Director (Jeffrey's boss's boss), he was deeply regretting the reports he had filed last year implicating his supervisor, Bob Jewel. He had not anticipated how the attention those reports attracted would endanger his own career.

As TSA's Security Director at Raleigh-Durham, Bob Jewel never did get the hang of things. A career bureaucrat with a reputation for integrity, he was perhaps the best example of what is known as the "Peter Principle." According to the Peter Principle, a person who is a good performer will be promoted up the career ladder until he reaches a position that is beyond his capabilities. That was Bob. There were many clues that Bob was in over his head, including a highly publicized security breach that resulted in more than 200 unscreened bags being placed on a flight to New York. Whether it was because of that embarrassment or due to the earlier complaints filed by Jeffrey against his inept boss, the TSA Professional Review Board (PRB) finally decided to look into things.

The PRB is the entity authorized to review alleged incidents of misconduct or mismanagement involving senior officials of TSA. When their review was completed, they notified Jeffrey of their intent to meet among themselves and eventually with Jeffrey about "serious issues that relate to you and your employment." That e-mail had come three weeks ago, leaving plenty of time for Jeffrey and his wife Elaine to imagine what would happen. As the meeting drew near, PRB investigator Drew Holly, an old friend, warned Jeffrey that he may need legal representation. Speaking strictly "off the record," Drew relayed a rumor that the PRB was seriously considering termination proceedings for both Jeffrey and Bob. These things were swirling around in Jeffrey's mind as he took a deep breath and cleaned his glasses.

Jeffrey knocked on Renaldo's door, but someone else answered. In fact, there were two people in the room Jeffrey did not recognize. Puzzled and growing more apprehensive, Jeffrey entered the office and sat down as Renaldo began to speak.

"Jeffrey, I'd like you to meet Thomas Muldoon and Kate O'Connor. Mr. Muldoon is TSA's Executive Officer for Employee Relations. Ms. O'Connor is also here from Washington, representing TSA's Legal Division. We have decided that both you and Bob Jewel should be relieved of your duties immediately." Jeffrey felt himself unable to move. Renaldo continued. "PRB has decided to issue a notice of proposed removal to you, and we are prepared to present the notice today."

"I see," said Jeffrey. "May I ask why?"

Then Thomas spoke.

"Before we get to that, Mr. Deck, I want you to think about another option we are putting on the table. We have determined that several gaps in leadership and management performance have developed here at Raleigh. But we recognize that you are not the only member of the management team. In fact, it is generally the case that the Security Director, not the Assistant Security Director, is most responsible for providing leadership. Therefore, we want to give you the benefit of the doubt in this matter. Ms. O'Connor has made a suggestion and it is one that I think has merit." With that, all three men turned and gave Kate O'Connor their attention.

"Mr. Deck," she began, "we have decided that in this case it would make sense to allow you to resign 'for personal reasons' at this time. If you agree that this option is the direction to go, we can prepare documents to that effect within the hour."

Jeffrey collected himself. "I don't understand," he said. "If Bob is responsible for the problems, why am I being terminated?"

"That's all in this letter, Mr. Deck," Kate replied as she pulled a sealed envelope from her satchel. "This letter of proposed removal specifies the justification for such an action."

"Can I see it?" asked Jeffrey.

"Honestly Mr. Deck, I would think you'd rather not see it. We are offering you a chance to resign for personal reasons before we issue the letter of proposed removal. Once you read it, you have been 'issued' the notice, and that means we must note in your file that very circumstance, leading to your resignation. We are trying to give you the option of avoiding professional embarrassment."

"Well, can you at least tell me what is in there, without issuing it to me?"

Then Thomas spoke again.

"Normally, if someone chooses to resign before the letter is issued, I am very careful not to let them see the letter. I think it is protective of the individual and the agency."

Kate chimed in, "You see, Mr. Deck, once you read the letter, you will have no choice but to resign in lieu of termination."

"Wait a minute," said Jeffrey. "You are saying that I must decide right now whether to resign for personal reasons, or resign anyway after being issued the letter of proposed removal, only in that case I would have the termination proposal on my record. But that would make me ineligible for another federal job, wouldn't it?"

"Yes," said Kate. "Those are your options."

"Well, I have another option, as you all know."

"Of course, Mr. Deck; you could fight the removal proposal," Kate acknowledged.

"That's right, I could. Therefore, I think I should have the right to know what the specific cause for termination is."

"As Mr. Muldoon has said, we prefer not to do it that way. Let's think of it like this," Kate summarized, "in exchange for sparing everyone the trouble of a lengthy, contested termination proceeding, we are offering you the chance to resign for personal reasons with a clean record."

Mr. Muldoon interjected once again. "Jeffrey, it's not like we are trying to pressure you here; but you know we are making a major shift in the management team. In fact, that's why Kate and I are in town today. We have a press release going out this afternoon about the management change, and we need to know how to characterize your departure."

Jeffrey was confused. He felt very much under pressure, and turned to Renaldo. "I don't know what to do, Mr. Wong. I've got twenty-two years in. I can't retire yet, and I don't want to throw everything away. And I still don't know why I am being terminated." Renaldo did not respond, so Jeffrey continued. "Listen everybody, let me talk to my attorney. It's Friday afternoon, and Monday is Memorial Day. Please give me until Tuesday to consider this. I really need the advice of my attorney."

"You have one hour, Mr. Deck," Kate insisted. "That gives you time to call your attorney or visit with the HR people if you like, and think it over. I'll prepare the resignation agreement."

"The HR people?" asked Jeffrey.

"Well," Kate replied, "as you know, if you are terminated you will sacrifice your health insurance and all other benefits as well. According to my information, you have 121 days of annual leave right now. If you resign for personal reasons, that would give you until the end of September before it takes effect. If you don't, you will be relieved of your duties effective immediately."

DISCUSSION QUESTIONS

1. Consider the information being given to Jeffrey by Kate O'Connor. How accurate are her assertions about Jeffrey's situation?
2. Is it true that Jeffrey has no right to see the letter before making his decision? Is Kate under any obligation to give accurate information to Jeffrey?
3. Evaluate the management styles of Renaldo, Kate, and Thomas. Why are they behaving this way? Are they handling the situation in the most effective way?

If Jeffrey does resign, could it ultimately be interpreted as an "involuntary" resignation or what is known as a constructive discharge? What would be the implications of this for TSA?

4. What should Jeffrey do? During his one hour, should he focus more on reaching his attorney, or on getting information from HR or other sources? What if he is unable to make contact with his attorney? Suppose no one in HR is available this hour. To what extent is Jeffrey's predicament his own fault?

Leading Public Organizations

CASE 7: GAY RIGHTS SIGNS ON CITY UTILITY POLES

The city council, which had been divided over the issue, finally adopted its new ordinance to regulate the kinds of messages allowed to go on city utility pole banners and bus benches. The original controversy had been sparked the previous summer when the Dakota Alliance for Tolerance and Acceptance (DATA) used the city's banner program to publicize its Gay Pride Festival and Parade. The new law specifically banned "social advocacy messages" or any "visual or textual communication that promotes political, ethnic, religious, or social advocacy organizations."

Mayor Roger Carvey was the leading proponent of the law. He had said in one of his many press conferences on the issue, "I am offended by DATA's incorporation of the symbol of Mount Rushmore under a rainbow. We all know what that rainbow signifies and it's disgusting!"

Other council members who supported the ordinance pointed out that if they didn't provide some regulation, then the Ku Klux Klan or some other hate group could promote their agenda using the banner program.

A local gay rights activist responded, "They act like they're preventing hate crimes with this new ordinance, but this new ordinance is itself a hate crime."

"Look, we are already regulating billboards in the city by prohibiting the advertisement of cigarettes, alcohol, and adult entertainment," said Mayor Carvey, "and this is no different."

The city attorney suggested that if the council wanted to avoid the political heat that comes with the responsibility of judging the appropriateness of banner messages, then they could turn over administration of the program to the utility companies through their lease agreements.

Over the mayor's objections, the rest of the city council voted to consider amending the new ordinance after receiving recommendations from the city manager's office.

City Manager Michael Hollingshead sighed when he heard that his office was the new custodian of what he called the "latest political hot potato."

Michael told close members among his staff, "Let's set up a committee of various city officials and community leaders to explore the issue. Hopefully, we can delay specific recommendations until this political storm blows over. Maybe even some of our current elected officials will have moved on by then."

DISCUSSION QUESTIONS

1. Is the idea suggested by the city attorney to delegate administration of the banner program to the utility companies a viable option? Why or why not? What would you recommend?

2. Is the new ordinance the moral equivalent of a hate crime? Regardless of whether or not you would support this kind of law, do you believe that it would survive judicial scrutiny? Explain.

3. What legitimate rationales, if any, would you consider to justify a city government's power to regulate the advertisement of such *legal* activities as smoking cigarettes, consuming alcohol, visiting strip clubs, or belonging to a gay pride association? What about the First Amendment rights to free speech and free association? Who should determine the standards of acceptability in these matters? Are there substantive differences among these activities that would suggest different approaches?

4. The strategy employed by the public officials in this case—both elected and appointed—is to delegate the immediate handling of this issue to some other entity. The city attorney recommends handing it over to private companies. The city council delegates it to the city manager. The city manager turns it over to an exploratory committee. What explains their behavior? When handling politically sensitive issues of this type, has anyone involved in this case performed in an unacceptable manner?

CASE 8: SERVING AT THE PLEASURE OF THE CITY COUNCIL

Granite, Texas is a small city of 10,000 people located thirty miles north of a major metropolitan area. The city has had a history of unstable city governance. At several points in the past, entire city councils had been recalled. City managers there have generally had unusually short tenures. Granite has struggled with financial problems for years due to a poor tax base. However, the city has recently been able to make some major improvements due in large part to a very innovative and popular city manager, Chuck Smith. With Smith's leadership, the city seemed to be progressing in a more positive direction. Smith and the council actively sought to improve the professionalism of the city by hiring more highly qualified individuals for key leadership positions in city government.

Under Smith's leadership, Granite received a 95 percent matching federal grant to make improvements to the city's airport. The airport project included extending the runway to 6,000 feet to make it jet accessible. In addition, a large number of new hangers were to be built—many of which could accommodate light aerospace industrial businesses the city hopes to attract. The final phase includes the construction of a new main terminal and hanger.

Smith was able to get the grant without any actual expenditure of city money by dedicating land the city already owned to meet the city's 5 percent matching contribution.

In addition to the airport project, the city also received several generous grants from the state to improve walkability in the city and modernize its infrastructure. These grants allowed the city to amend its budget and make more capital improvement to its water and sewer lines as well as installing new sidewalks and starting a trail system.

Smith recently resigned to take another position at a large city in Wyoming. Many of the projects were well underway or near completion when Smith accepted the new position. As a result, the council sought an experienced city manager who could help the city complete the projects. In the interim, the council appointed Janet Homes acting city manager. Homes had served as Smith's closest advisor and the city's human resources director. Homes did a good job as interim and kept all the projects, including the airport project, moving forward and on schedule.

The council interviewed several well-qualified candidates for the position. During the interviews, members of the council were very clear with candidates that the city had a good team and they were not looking for anyone to come in and "rock the boat." All of the candidates interviewed made it clear they thought the current management team was great, and that they would not have a problem working with the current staff.

The council felt that although all of the interviews had gone well, the candidate John Bramante was the best qualified. The council extended Mr. Bramante a very competitive offer and he accepted.

At first, everything seemed to be going well. John spent his first few weeks getting to know everyone and appeared to be learning the organizational culture.

However, after three months on the job, John began to make a number of troubling changes. He ordered new office furniture in spite of the fact that the city hall and all its furniture were brand new. He also implemented a new purchasing procedure and announced on a number of occasions to staff and citizens alike that, "We need to turn some things upside down around here."

A week after changing the purchasing policy, John called all the department heads together for a staff meeting. At the meeting, John announced, "We need to make some dramatic changes in this organization. I need people that I can trust and work closely with to get things done around here. So, I have decided that from this point forward Janet Homes will be strictly limited to handling human resources. I am fully taking on all of the current capital projects and Janet will no longer have any responsibility in this area. Melody Clark will no longer be purchasing agent and will be reassigned to the city clerk's office to handle accounts payable, and Police Chief Tom Jones will now be assigned the position of Director of Public Safety and oversee both police and fire departments. These changes are effective immediately."

The new assignments took all the employees by surprise. The lack of a transition period caused many of the capital projects to slow down. Because of employee complaints, the council intervened and asked John what was going on. Two councilmen, Jason Stone and Brad Begley, began to demand answers from John regarding the reassignment of duties at city hall. John replied that it was not the councilmen's prerogative to question the day-to-day operation of the city government, but rather it was their job to set "general policy and nothing more."

Two weeks later, Councilman Begley requested that the possible termination of the city manager be placed on the council's agenda for an executive session.

DISCUSSION QUESTIONS

1. In a council/manager type system of government, the city manager is responsible for the daily operation of the city. To what extent should he or she be free to reorganize and restructure staff and operations? Should he or she advise the council first?
2. Given the fact that John was hired with the understanding that he would "not rock the boat," was it ethical for him to accept the job and then engage in a major reorganization?
3. Should Councilman Begley have sought to work with John to reach an understanding or compromise before placing his possible termination on a public document? Could Councilman Begley's action signal to staff that the council doesn't have to respect the decisions of a city manager?
4. As citizens, should city employees be able to contact council members about their concerns, or does their employment with the city constrain their First Amendment rights to free speech and petition of government for redress of grievances?

CASE 9: OFFICE OF EMERGENCY MANAGEMENT FAKE PRESS CONFERENCE

The State of California is prone to periodic droughts. During times of drought, the state often experiences outbreaks of wildfires. Shifting, high winds hamper the ability to control such wildfires.

The Office of Emergency Services (OES) is an agency that plays a critical role in the management of disasters such as earthquakes and wildfires. The mission statement of the department reads:

> The OES mission is to ensure the state is ready and able to mitigate against, prepare for, respond to, and recover from the effects of emergencies that threaten lives, property, and the environment. OES coordinates the activities of all state agencies relating to preparation and implementation of the State Emergency Plan. OES also coordinates the response efforts of state and local agencies to ensure maximum effect with minimum overlap and confusion. Additionally, OES coordinates the integration of federal resources into state and local responses and recovery operations. OES accomplishes this mission through programs and outreach efforts that assist local and state government in their emergency management efforts.

Last year, wildfires were particularly bad. Over twenty wildfires raged from north of Santa Barbara all the way down to the Mexican border. Wildfires destroyed over 1,900 homes, burned almost 600,000 acres, and killed twenty-two people. The entire community of Cuyamaca was destroyed in one day as the Santa Ana winds drove the fire.

After two weeks of battling the fires, firefighters were exhausted and the citizens and press in California were becoming critical of OES's response. Reporters and citizens began questioning OES's effectiveness in coordinating efforts among state and local agencies. The governor was also criticized for the delay in declaring a state of emergency and requesting federal assistance. In fact, OES was following a detailed plan and fairly effectively managing resources. The extreme drought and high wind conditions proved to be overwhelming challenges.

As criticism intensified, OES Public Affairs Director, Phil Jones, called a press conference to explain how OES was managing the crisis. OES notified the press 15 minutes prior to the press conference and said that anyone who could not make it to the OES headquarters could call in and listen to the conference. However, the call-in line was a listen-only line.

OES's Deputy Administrator, Mike Johnson, opened the conference with a brief overview of the current situation and OES's role and efforts in coordinating federal, state, and local agencies. No reporters had yet arrived after Johnson concluded his opening remarks. Phil then signaled his staff to begin asking Johnson questions. They obliged by throwing several "softball" questions.

Media Liaison, Betty Beal, asked, "Has OES sent enough commodities to shelters in the affected area?"

Johnson replied, "We have. OES has shipped hundreds of thousands of items to more than forty-five shelters to ensure that there is enough food to care for those who are seeking shelter."

Deputy Public Affairs Director, Paul Hampshire, asked, "What does it mean to have the Governor declare a state of emergency?"

"Well, the Governor's declaration in effect signals the federal government to get involved and hopefully send help and funds through FEMA." said Johnson.

Thomas Lair, another OES public affairs staffer, asked, "I understand the Governor and OES Administrator are going out there today. What is their objective? And is anyone else traveling with them?"

"The Governor and Administrator are going out there to show their support—to let the people of California know that this administration is taking this situation seriously, and that we are committed to getting this whole thing under control. Also, they'll talk with affected individuals to see what kind of help they need. This is a good show of support. And yes, others will be traveling with the Governor, including his Chief of Staff and our state's Secretary of Homeland Security," replied Johnson.

Phil, from the side of the room, then said, "Okay folks, last question." Johnson pointed back at Beal who asked, "Are you proud of OES's response so far?"

"Look, we have a very difficult situation here. OES staff members have been working around the clock coordinating agencies and following our emergency management plan. We have executed the plan efficiently and effectively. We've made modifications to the plan as needed since every situation is unique. We've been responsive and sensitive to this situation. Our policies and procedures allow for maximum coordination and minimal overlap of efforts. So, yes, I am proud of the job we're doing here at OES. Thank you all and good day."

Within a couple of hours, the press caught on that the news conference had been faked. Reporters began calling Jones demanding to know why he had staged the fake conference. Phil replied, "We didn't stage a fake conference. When it became apparent that none of the press corps was going to make it, we simply had staff ask questions that we've been receiving from the press itself."

Pressure mounted. CNN, among others, sent reporters to OES Administrator Mike McConnell's office demanding to know if he knew about the fake press conference and if he had approved of such a tactic.

McConnell's office released a statement that said that the Administrator did not know of the fake conference in advance and that his office would not have approved of such a technique. The individuals involved were being placed on administrative leave pending the outcome of an internal investigation. The release also said OES was working on a policy to ensure that such an incident did not occur in the future.

The Governor's office also released a statement disavowing any knowledge prior to the event. It said the Governor would never condone such a practice.

Three weeks after the conference, McConnell fired Phil and reinstated all other employees who had been placed on administrative leave.

DISCUSSION QUESTIONS

1. Was it unethical for Phil Jones to "stage" a fake news conference? What ethical theory might justify such a decision? Which ethical theories would say the faked new conference was unethical? Is it ever appropriate to manipulate the media to maximize the positive impact on a public agency's public relations? If so, what alternatives to a faked news conference might be more acceptable?

2. Should the other employees have refused to go along with Jones's request that they play the part of reporters? Why or why not? Should they have "blown the whistle" on Jones prior to the event? Why or why not?

3. Was Phil's punishment appropriate or was it too harsh? Since other employees did go along with Jones's idea, should they have been punished as well? What about Deputy Administrator Mike Johnson? Justify your answer.

4. Even though they are operated by private companies, do news organizations have an obligation to serve the public by explaining the challenges faced by public agencies in this type of situation? Or do they have a higher duty to make the news more interesting in order to attract larger audiences and thereby maximize the profits of their investors?

CASE 10: SQUEEZING OUT THE GARBAGE COLLECTORS

City Manager Laura Hamilton looked across the table at the union's representatives. "We're done here. The labor contract expires at midnight and I am recommending to the city council that we go ahead with our plan to privatize the city's solid waste collection services." She stood up and began placing papers in her brief case.

"Hold on Laura!" exclaimed Cameron Fitzgerald, the Staff Director for the local chapter of the Association of City Employees (ACE) union, but he knew he had lost the war. Even though he believed management had cherry picked the data to present the absolute best-case scenario for privatization, he knew that persuading city council and even the public would be nearly impossible in the face of these overly rosy projections. Still, he wanted to salvage as much as possible for the blue-collar employees he represented. "The very least you could do is to implement your plan in stages so that my members can make the necessary preparations. Let me remind you these are also *your* employees who have dedicated years of their lives to this city. It's the least you can do."

Laura paused as if in deep thought. This was the opening she had gambled on, but she didn't want to seem too eager. "I think I might have a way of delaying full implementation of our plan. If you are agreeable, we could retain a full third of the solid waste workforce next fiscal year. If the city employees prove themselves competitive head to head against a private company both in terms of cost and services provided, we could keep them on indefinitely. And as for the remaining two-thirds of the employees, they can keep their jobs for the remainder of this fiscal year while they look for other opportunities either within city employment or outside."

Cameron smiled hesitantly. "I believe that we have an agreement in principle."

"Great," Laura said, "I'll get the papers ready for signatures by the morning."

As they were leaving the building, Laura's assistant caught up to her and asked, "Why did you cave like that? They were just where you wanted them."

"No, I got what I wanted all along," Laura explained. "You see, every ten years or so, the sanitation workers go on strike and the city has no recourse but to wait it out until the citizens complain long and hard enough for us to give in to the union's excessive demands. We have in effect broken the back of this union. But the city's solid waste workers can still be useful. I envision dividing up the city into two districts. Starting next July, the city's much-reduced Solid Waste Division will take over one half of the city. We'll farm out the other half to a waste management vendor. Then we'll play them against each other. If the city's solid waste employees threaten to strike, we'll say 'fine' because we have contractors not only willing, but hungry to step in and take their place. And if the contractor gets greedy in the bidding process, we can always say 'fine' because we can perform these services with our own employees. We accomplish half the work with only a third of the employees. Meanwhile the ACE union lives on officially representing our civilian workforce. It won't have any real power, but it should discourage other more powerful unions from coming in to fill the vacuum."

DISCUSSION QUESTIONS

1. How much weight should be given to taking care of employees who have worked for the city for years?
2. Is Laura's plan to pit city workers against private contractors justified by the projected cost savings and potential strikes prevented? How should the data be gathered to determine cost savings and service levels? What are the advantages and disadvantages to privatizing the solid waste function?
3. Describe Laura's leadership style. Is it effective? In this instance, what is her primary strategy for motivating employees? What are her underlying assumptions relevant to the management-labor relationship? Would you like to serve under Laura's leadership? Why or why not?
4. Given the circumstances, has Cameron negotiated the best deal possible for his union membership?

CASE 11: THE GOVERNOR'S TRANSITION TEAM

David Walker had just been elected as the new governor of the state. Although his inauguration would not take place until January, the state legislature had allocated funds to cover the costs of transition. The state agencies began making their adjustments in anticipation of a new executive administration from a different political party.

As a Personnel Specialist in the state Office of Human Resources, Nathan Hayes noticed some changes going on around his agency. The most visible was the transfer of Melissa Welch, the Training Director from the state Department of Health and Human Services. She took over a new position as Principal Assistant to the Administrator of the Office of Human Resources. Nathan later learned that she was in fact the incoming governor's choice to be the new Administrator over Human Resources and that she was in charge of vetting all candidates for the governor's new political appointments.

Nathan was intrigued but he didn't have much time to concern himself with what he considered to be the typical power play at the top levels of state government. He and other members in his division had their hands full managing the extremely heavy human resources workload. But Nathan was bothered that in spite of this wave of increased activity, several staff members in his team had been reassigned to other projects. It was not only a mystery but it was also beginning to be a matter of some concern.

Later that day, Nathan found himself in the elevator with one of his coworkers who had been temporarily reassigned to some other project. So he asked, "Jennifer, what are all of you working on?"

She said, "We're providing staff support for David Walker's incoming administration. Specifically, I am screening applications for appointments to various boards and commissions."

As Nathan was commuting home that evening, he heard on the radio that Governor-elect David Walker and his team had gotten themselves in a bit of political hot water when they failed to reimburse the Department of Tourism for use of a limousine. Apparently, Walker was supposed to use his transition funds to cover the costs of official transportation. His political supporters in Tourism, on the other hand, were trying to help him "conserve" the specially designated transition funding by charging the costs of the vehicle to regular agency line item accounts. It was a minor political scandal that was easily explained by the confusion surrounding the transition and by overeager political supporters among the state workforce.

Nathan then connected the dots. In his own agency, regular state employees who were supposed to be conducting normal state business had been reassigned quietly to handle the business of the transition team. The agency was getting behind in all of its regular work. Nathan all but knew that their salaries were not being reimbursed by transition funds.

DISCUSSION QUESTIONS

1. Should Nathan call the local media to investigate? Should he gather more facts before he decides whether or not to do so? Should he expect to receive special protections as a whistleblower?
2. What other options should Nathan consider? How would you recommend Nathan react to this situation?
3. Should Nathan's personal politics influence his decision? In other words, if he in fact voted for Walker to be governor, would it be more ethically defensible for him to maintain his silence about the possible problem?
4. The regular turnover in elected administrations is a routine challenge for the public service. The bureaucracy is in fact charged with being responsive to its political masters. At the same time, each agency must also meet its legally mandated mission. How should career public administrators best maintain the balance between these two conflicting responsibilities? How can one recognize when a line has been crossed?

CASE 12: RUNNING THE NUMBERS AT THE STATE HEALTH DEPARTMENT

Henry Paxton, a Statistician for the State Health Department, was feeling rather restless late one Thursday morning. He found his job dull and uneventful. He was always running the same old formulas and punching in the same old numbers. A commercial from the radio that sat on Henry's desk inspired him to relieve his boredom. On a break, he decided to approach Bob Hicks, a fellow employee in the Records Division. He said, "Bob, I'm going down to the new racetrack at lunchtime to put some money on a horse and I was wondering if you wanted me to place a bet for you too?"

Bob whipped out his wallet and gave Henry $10. He told Henry, "Just put this on the nose of the same horse you're bettin' on."

Henry went down to the track during his lunch period and put Bob's money and $10 of his own on a horse with a long shot to win. He quickly went back to the agency. As he worked that afternoon he listened for the race results on the radio. At the end of the day, Henry came up to Bob with a big smile on his face. "Bob, you're one hundred dollars richer today!"

Bob was pleased and both felt lucky. So the next day, they repeated their performance. Sally Buchanan heard about what they were doing and decided to join them in their wager. Once again, they bet on a long shot and it came through. Each one shared $75 in winnings.

For the next four weeks, the trio would play the horses from work every Thursday and Friday afternoon. Their initial luck was extended by a computer program that Henry developed at home which would compute the statistics and project the probable winners of each race. Word spread throughout the organization of their string of successes. More and more people were willing to risk a few dollars for a chance to win big money. The gambling activities soon included most of the technical/clerical support staff and several of the professional staff. Henry's office soon looked like a revolving door as workers from various department streamed in to cover bets. A few employees, such as Martin Baughman, did not participate due to religious reasons. He sometimes received good-natured teasing from his coworkers to join in the fun, but he just shrugged them off. At one point, nobody had won a specialized bet called the "Pick Six" for several days. The rollover fund associated with it carried an amount in excess of $6 million. Martin, despite his own religious convictions, sheepishly approached Henry, and said, "If you don't mind, I'm giving you a few dollars to bet for me on the horses."

Henry was surprised but pleased. He asked, "Martin, I thought this went against your religion."

"It does, but with that much money, I just didn't want to be the only person to show up for work in our office tomorrow if the pool actually won."

Meanwhile, Dr. Quaid Jefferson, the Division Director over Vital Statistics, noticed a marked decrease in output from his department. A corresponding increase in the error rate was also evidenced. Not a man to often become involved with his lower-ranking professional employees, he felt that this matter was too significant to ignore. He made discreet inquiries from his own secretary and others that he trusted. They made him aware of the continuing and growing involvement of a number of his workers in betting the ponies at the local track. Dr. Jefferson's secretary advised him not to take the betting too seriously. She said that the workers only gambled on their breaks and at lunchtime and that it didn't interfere with their work. "Besides," she pointed out, "you have participated every year since you've been here in the annual football pool and that's technically illegal, while horse-betting is not against the law in this jurisdiction. Furthermore, everybody knows our Administrator, Dr. Tom Carmines, takes every Friday afternoon off to go to the racetrack."

Dr. Jefferson was persuaded but not convinced. The numbers he saw indicated that the activities were lowering productivity. He was also worried about the image of the agency should the public find out. He felt it prudent to prepare a memo prohibiting gambling during working hours for the Administrator's signature. He hand-delivered the memo to Dr. Carmines and said, "I feel you, as the administrator of this agency, should sign this memo and have it distributed to every employee in the Health Department as soon as possible."

Dr. Carmines accepted the memo and replied, "I'll certainly consider it . . . thank you." After Dr. Jefferson left his office, the Administrator read the prepared memo, crumpled it up in his hand, and threw it in a nearby wastebasket.

DISCUSSION QUESTIONS

1. What constitutes working hours? Is an employee's lunch hour a work hour? Does your answer depend on whether or not the employee is paid through lunch or if they are salaried? If the situation above involved drinking at lunch rather than betting, would your answer change?
2. Is it ethical for state employees to participate in a football pool that is illegal? Does Dr. Jefferson have a double standard since he does participate in the football pool?
3. What if Henry Paxton had developed the betting program on his office computer but on his own time after hours? Would this act be ethical? What if other employees were given permission to use their computers for other personal issues after working hours?
4. Dr. Jefferson suspects that the gambling activities are affecting work productivity. How would he go about establishing a direct correlation to prove his assertion?

Public Financial Management and Budgeting

CASE 13: THE LONG FORGOTTEN RAISE IN THE PROPERTY TAX

Edward Brecher opened the revenue estimate reports. He expected the picture to be grim, but he wasn't prepared for the severity of these negative numbers. He had been City Manager for less than a year and after reviewing the figures he was already daydreaming about resigning. Then reality hit him: He really needed this job. Jill Caravan, his Finance Director, knocked on his open office door and stepped in.

"Ed, you got a minute?"

"Sure, come on in."

"You asked me to research any possible new revenue sources and I think I found something." Her not-so-subtle smile hinted at optimism.

"I'm assuming you have good news."

"I do!" she said. "Look here. Twelve years ago, before you and I ever worked for the city, the voters passed a significant increase in the local property tax."

"Okay . . . so, what does this mean?"

"They approved the tax, but it was never implemented. Our attorneys have told me that according to state law and our own charter, we would be legally justified in proceeding ahead with full implementation."

Brecher smiled for a brief moment until seriousness once again returned to his face. "We may be on solid ground legally, but if we implemented the tax increase at this time, it would be political suicide. The voters would revolt and the council would have my head. This is just one more example of the long train of oversights and screw-ups the last administration left as a legacy. Because of their excesses, we're going to have to work long and hard to rebuild people's trust. And that won't happen overnight. It's a great idea but we just can't think about something like that at this time."

Caravan responded, "We're running out of options and there's not much left to do but take deep cuts in personnel and pull back on the services we offer. Think about it before you make up your mind. I bet we could increase the tax a little this year with nobody noticing. If it did get the public's attention, I'm sure we could frame it in a politically palatable way."

"I think you're being a bit naive," Brecher said, "but I'll sleep on it. Let me have your documentation to review."

DISCUSSION QUESTIONS

1. Would it be ethical for the manger to implement the "forgotten tax" without discussing it with the city council? Why or why not?
2. Since the citizens already voted on the tax, should the city begin collecting it without a press release? What about phasing it in slowly over time?
3. Should the city conduct a poll to see if citizens would prefer to have the approved tax implemented or services cut? Should politicians and civil servants always follow the wishes of citizens, or should officials (who often have a higher level of knowledge) exercise their own judgment in such situations? Is it "undemocratic" for officials to ignore public opinion? If citizens feel their wishes are being ignored, what recourse do they have? Should all states allow for more citizen participation through devices such as initiative petition, referendum, and recall elections?
4. Should the tax be put up again for a revote?

CASE 14: TUITION REIMBURSEMENT PROGRAM

The city's union negotiations were not going well. They were already operating without a current contract. The long afternoon session would surely stretch until at least the early evening. Kristy Streib, the Chief Negotiator for the management team, requested a break. She walked down the hallway and got out her cell phone. She placed the previously scheduled call to Hank Alvarez, the Human Resources Director.

"Hi Kris, how's it going?" Hank sounded upbeat as he answered the phone.

"Not so great," Kristy said. "The union's not buying into any of this total compensation business. They won't give an inch on benefits. Obviously they want to maintain their current package of health insurance and negotiate only on salary."

"Have you and your team trotted out the statistics on how much more health insurance is costing the city now?"

"Yeah. They weren't even impressed by the rapid acceleration in prescription costs," Kristy continued, "and they want the same good deal that police and fire got."

"That's never going to happen in this jurisdiction," Hank said. "Our city council is always going to back our officers and firefighters. What about the tuition reimbursement program?"

"They laughed at us. They said that the tuition reimbursement program benefits the city more than it benefits the general pay plan employee."

"Take it off the table then. Tell them that the tuition reimbursement program is hereby discontinued. We'll resurrect a similar plan for the management employees in a couple of weeks. That should rattle their cages. Maybe their membership will push to get it back and we can use it for leverage next year."

Two days later, Jim Gill, who coordinated the city's tuition reimbursement program, answered his phone.

"Jim, this is Hank. We're going to need to discontinue the tuition reimbursement program immediately. Unless they're already enrolled and have been attending classes, we'll need to stop providing any more educational assistance."

"Wow . . . what's going on?" Jim asked.

"The union for the general pay plan employees will not recognize tuition aid as a benefit."

"Why?"

"The real reason is that they don't want to recognize it as a benefit that's up for negotiation. They say that it's really in the best interest of the city more than the employee. As proof, they point to the requirement that whatever course is supported by the city has to be job related. Now, don't worry Jim, we're going to resurrect the program soon, but we'll offer it only to the management pay plan employees," Hank said. "And this time, we'll do like we did with police and fire, and let them enroll in anything they like."

Jim followed through and dutifully closed up the tuition reimbursement program. A couple of months later, the new Performance Enhancement Through Education (PETE) program was initiated for management employees only. It paralleled similar programs in the police and fire departments. The only requirement for tuition reimbursement was that the management employee take it through an accredited university. Tuition would be reimbursed only as high as the highest tuition for a local public university at the appropriate level for lower- and upper-division undergraduate and graduate courses. The new program was marketed to the management employees as a new benefit. It would in effect replace the annual longevity bonus which was frozen for existing employees and discontinued for new employees. In short, it was a consolation offered to employees who would lose future increases in compensation for length of service.

Shortly into the new program, the PETE committee met to allocate the tuition among the several applications. There was more than enough money to meet all of the requests for the current fiscal year. All applications met the minimum requirements of college credit offered through accredited programs. Two applications in particular caused some discussion among the PETE committee as "not being relevant to the job," but Jim explained that as it was a benefit, the employee should have much more flexibility in taking whatever courses interested him or her.

Since the start of the program, Hank Alvarez had left the city and was replaced as Human Resources Director by Dana Bartlett. Dana had been familiar with the old tuition reimbursement program, but was surprised to find out that, in her new role as HR Director, she would be the signatory of the reformatted program. Her approval was required for funds to be dispensed to those management employees seeking tuition assistance under PETE. She accepted all the recommendations of the PETE committee, until she read the same two applications that had generated discussion among the original PETE committee members. She quickly got on her telephone.

"Jim, I need you to come to my office immediately."

"Be right there."

When Jim arrived, he found his new director reading through the PETE applications with a visible frown.

"Jim, I want you to sit down," she pointed to a chair in front of her desk. "Explain to me how you and your committee could possibly have let this request for a language course in Kiswahili and another course here on how to start your own Internet business be approved. I don't see either one being relevant to the job here. I've never even heard of Kiswahili and I doubt that we have many Kiswahilians here in our state."

"Well, um, first of all Kiswahili, as I understand, is just another name for Swahili," Jim gently offered, ". . . you know, Swahili, it's the official language of Africa—no, what I mean is that it's become the lingua franca of the African continent."

"Whatever, Jim. You get my point. We don't have much need for our city employees to learn Swahili here in the Midwest. Why not Spanish? We have a growing Hispanic population. What about American Sign Language? We always need interpreters. I just can't remember the last time we had any call for Swahili or Kiswahili in these parts," Dana said sarcastically.

"As you may remember, when the new PETE program was reconstituted from its previous incarnation as the city tuition reimbursement program, it was sold to management employees as a benefit. Your predecessor and the former city manager expressly said that we would drop any requirement that a course had to be related to an employee's current job. Frankly, I didn't think we had any choice but to approve this application."

"Then what about this one—how to open up your own Internet business? I bet you this is all about eBay or some scam. We don't want our employees diverting their attention from their city jobs and start exploring other careers. You've got to be kidding me. I'm not going to defend this when it hits the papers."

"Once again, Ms. Bartlett, the committee felt it had no choice. We did pause on both of these applications, but according to the way the program was set up and how it's been sold to the employees, we're supposed to approve this course. It's offered at the city community college for college credit and it's all accredited by the appropriate authorities."

"Well, I want you to march yourself back down to your office and write a rejection letter to both of these individuals. You say whatever you like that's polite and official, but make sure you include the statement that their requests are being sent back because any approval would be against the best interests of the city," Dana commanded. She reached across her desk and called her secretary to ask her next appointment to come in.

Jim left her office and headed back downstairs.

DISCUSSION QUESTIONS

1. Should the city pay for courses that are not directly relevant to an employee's job? Even if the requirement was that the course should be relevant to one's job, isn't that still a benefit to the employee?
2. Was it ethical for the city to give the tuition assistance to management as a method of pressuring the union into accepting it as a benefit?
3. Was it ethical for Dana to change a policy on her own initiative without recommending a formal policy change? Who should have the power to set formal policy for a city? Given the fact that a committee of the city had already discussed this matter and approved it, was it ethical for Dana to override the decision of the committee on her own initiative? If not, what exactly is her role as approving signatory?
4. What should Jim do in this situation? Should he circumvent his boss in this situation and bring the matter up with the city manager? Why or why not? If Jim follows Dana's orders and denies the tuition request, what recourse should the employees who have relied on the policy have to protest the decision? Does your answer depend on whether or not the courses have already been taken in anticipation of them being paid for?

CASE 15: SUBMITTING AN INCOMPLETE FINANCIAL REPORT

City Treasurer Phyllis Colvin looked at all the statements again as she was preparing the Excel spreadsheet for that night's council meeting. The figures were not adding up. She was short $10,000 in the general fund. She was reasonably sure that the money had been transferred accidentally into one of the other operating accounts or perhaps into the public works account. She just couldn't find it, and it was only 30 minutes before she was due to give her quarterly financial report to the council.

As she sat there wondering where in the world the money could have been transferred to, an idea crossed her mind. She could report the $10,000 as accounted for to the council and then worry about finding it in the morning when she had more time and less stress.

DISCUSSION QUESTIONS

1. What justification can be used to defend Phyllis's action should she decide to falsely report the money as accounted for?
2. What ethical theory would conclude that Phyllis should not file a false report, and why?
3. What would you do in this situation and why?
4. If we take for granted that the money has just been accidentally transferred (and that there is no chance that it has been illegally misappropriated), does that change your answers?

CASE 16: INELIGIBLE FOR SUGGESTION SYSTEM AWARDS

The Productivity Enhancement Program (PEP) was a newly legislated suggestion system for state employees. The PEP program rewarded state employees who came up with innovative ideas that either produced more revenue or resulted in measurable cost savings. The legislature—with its ever-present concern that some bureaucrat somewhere might scam the system—placed some fairly severe constraints on the program. Not only did an employee have to come up with an idea, but he or she had to also see the idea through to full implementation. The employee could then receive a percentage of the documented savings (or revenue increase) for the first year of implementation, up to a maximum reward of $7,500. Another limitation was that an employee could only be rewarded for proposing an idea that was not a part of their regular job.

Jonah Daniels was assigned to be the coordinator of the program. He answered to the PEP Committee which was composed of several political appointees. The role of the PEP Committee was to make final approval of any monies to be disbursed for rewards. Jonah knew that the program needed some early successes. Giving deserving state employees some highly visible rewards would be critical for ensuring the program's long-term viability. He was pleased to find on his desk what he thought would be a worthy application.

Melana Armstrong worked as the Agency Auditor for the State Commerce Department. On weekends, she was involved with a prison ministry sponsored by her church. She had noticed prisoners making telephone calls to family and friends on the outside. Cell phones were strictly prohibited. Prisoners were restricted to making collect calls only, from pay phones available during limited times for just that purpose.

She called an agency auditor for the Department of Corrections and mentioned her idea:

"I've checked the records and these prisoners are making phone calls under an arrangement with a long distance carrier that hasn't changed for years.

The company charges more for these collect calls from pay phones than for any other type of call. The state allows this phone company to place its pay phones in its facilities, but the state doesn't get a cut. I suggest that we contact the company and ask for the state's share of the profits."

So prison officials shortly thereafter contacted the phone company and asked for the state's cut. At first, the company balked. When prison management threatened to get the company to take out the pay phones and give the business to a competitor, the company relented and gave the state a hefty share of the profits. The documented revenue and cost savings for the first year was over $2 million.

Jonah confirmed the information provided on the application and recommended to the committee that Melana should receive the full reward allowed, the maximum $7,500. Gerald White, who as the State Director of Finance was appointed to the PEP Committee, immediately registered his objection. He said, "I am reading here from the job description for the agency auditor classification and it states that one of the primary duties for this position is to 'review and analyze the work processes, accounting procedures, and business practices of the agency to enhance performance and encourage efficiency.' Therefore, she cannot be eligible for this reward because it's part of her regular duties."

Betty Cox who was chairing the committee shook her head. "Gerry, you can't be serious. She's an auditor for Commerce, not Corrections."

"As you know, I'm an auditor by profession and I'm telling you this is already part of her professional responsibilities. The job description does not specify which state agency. She only did what she's already supposed to do. That's clear. Let's move on to consider the next one."

DISCUSSION QUESTIONS

1. How should Jonah respond?
2. Would it make a difference that Melana's idea was inspired while she was off duty? Does it make a difference that her idea was inspired at another agency?
3. Since this is a new program, the initial decisions taken by the PEP Committee will serve as precedents for future situations. In that light, should the final decision be more permissive or restrictive? Which one will best ensure future success of the program? Explain your rationale.
4. As chair, how should Betty best resolve this issue to maintain cordial relations among committee members, support staff, and award nominees while simultaneously acting as watchdog over public monies?

CASE 17: FREE BOAT FOR SODA DISPLAY AT STATE LODGE

Reggie Tolson had served as the camp store supervisor for the State Lodge at Lake Sandstone for the past three seasons. His salary was low but he was allowed to stay in one of the cabins for free and receive complimentary meals in the Lodge restaurant. The big advantage was that he enjoyed the job itself and, he was able to fish and golf during his off hours.

Deena Gibson had come down from the state office earlier in the week to let him know that they really needed him to increase the revenue during the forthcoming season. The legislators were once again threatening to close down the lodge because it couldn't seem to get through an entire fiscal year without needing some major injection of state monies. She explained that the lodge was expected to at least make enough money to be self-sustaining. She had suggested raising prices on most of the store products since there was no real competition from other stores for miles around.

"They should have to pay a premium for convenience," she rationalized.

Deena had also recommended that he engage in some promotional campaigns to increase traffic through the shop. He was still hoping to generate some ideas when the local soft drink vendor came to talk.

"Reg, I have a proposition for you," he said. "If you'll let my company build a display right here in the front of the store we can increase your sales volume at least 400 percent. You can't lose, because if we don't, we'll eat the difference."

"What kind of display are we talking about?"

"Okay, imagine this. Starting on Memorial Day weekend—the start of the season—we place a small fishing boat right here at the front of the store. We'll tilt it up on its side like so and then fill it with twenty-four-pack cases of our soft drinks. We'll offer a special promotional price. The small difference you might lose per item will be more than made up by increased volume. You'll also find that the campers and lodgers will end up buying other items as well. Especially don't forget to stock up on coolers and ice."

"That sounds like a good deal," Reggie said, "but let me talk it over with my supervisor and get her okay."

"Great," the vendor said, "but I haven't even told you the best part. At the end of the promotional cycle which should be about nine or ten days—we'll at least get two weekends with the display—I'll come back and pick up any residual product that's not sold, but I won't pick up the fishing boat. It's small, but it's a beauty. It's made out of fiberglass and is sturdy as hell. We'll even throw in a couple of paddles and some fishing gear, you know, for display purposes. You can do whatever with the boat after we're through."

"All right, let me check with my supervisor and get back to you."

"Just call me on my cell phone when you can, and we'll get you set up right away."

Reggie realized that he could make better money at many other summer jobs, but it was perks like this boat offer that kept him coming back year after year. Still, he was concerned about the propriety of taking such a valuable gift. He really did want the boat. Finally, he called Deena and told her about the offer. He didn't know how she would react but was surprised when she said, "We really need the extra sales, so it sounds like a good idea. And Reg, I won't be able to come out to the lake very often, but I'm hoping that when I do, you'll let me take your new boat out for the day once in a while."

DISCUSSION QUESTIONS

1. Now that Reggie has secured his supervisor's blessing on the deal, is it ethical for him to accept the soft drink display offer?
2. Should Reggie make inquiries further up his chain of command to make sure that he would be on solid ground accepting the boat? Should Reggie investigate further to see if there is an official means to add the boat to the state lodge inventory?
3. Has the soft drink vendor offering the deal made any ethical transgressions?
4. Would this offer by the soft drink vendor generate the same level of ethical concern if Reggie worked for a private sector employer?

CASE 18: CHARGING FOR COPIES OF PUBLIC DOCUMENTS

City Manager Troy Jones was looking at yet another stack of requests for the production of public documents from members of the local press. The city was in financial trouble, and the press was taking advantage of the crisis to sell newspapers. As a result, the three major papers in town had each filed multiple requests for thousands of documents to try and find any hint of impropriety. The problem with these requests was that they were taking up a huge amount of the city staff's time, and further exasperating the financial problems of the city since it was costing money in terms of employee hours spent searching for and then copying the requested documents.

The city was charging the press 3 cents per page for the copies in accordance with the city's current copy rate schedule, but this was not even covering the actual cost of just the copies themselves. Because the city had been on a tight budget for the past five years, it had not purchased new copiers in many years. Most of the city's copiers were more than ten years old, and maintenance coupled with supply costs meant that the actual cost of producing copies was about 15 cents per page, not including the cost in employee wages for those making the copies. As a result of these costs, Troy was at his wit's end. The city could not continue to make these copies, and besides these requests were really nothing more than a fishing expedition in his opinion.

City Attorney Randal Shadid had been with the city for over fifteen years, and Troy trusted his counsel, so one day in Randal's office he asked Randal for his advice on how to curb all of these open records requests.

Randal replied, "I understand your problem. I have seen all the requests, and I agree they are getting excessive. It seems to me that I remember something in the state statute about being able to charge an hourly fee for search time that an employee spends on such requests. Let me look into it and get back with you in a couple of days."

The next day Randal looked at the statute and found the language he was looking for in Title 22 S.S. § 1051, which was the State's Open Records Act. It read in part:

> Each state agency or political subdivision shall make all its records
> open and available for public inspection and copying unless such

records are specifically exempted by subsection (B) below. Provided, however, that each agency or political subdivision can charge a reasonable copying fee not to exceed the actual cost of the copies. In addition to the copying fee, an agency or political subdivision may charge a reasonable research fee to cover administrative expenses on requests that are overly large or burdensome.

Randal then did a search on the city's ordinance regarding the copying fee schedule and discovered that the ordinance originally set the copying fee at 3 cents, but that it provided that the city manager could from time to time adjust the fee schedule to deal with increased costs. Randal reported his findings to Troy.

Based on Randal's report, Troy decided to initiate a change in the fee schedule to increase the cost of copies to 15 cents and to charge a $45 an hour fee on each and every request for production of documents for any staff research time that was spent finding the documents and actually copying. Troy was sure that, with the new fee schedule in place, the press would slow down their absurd production requests.

DISCUSSION QUESTIONS

1. Even though the statute and the ordinance seem to give Troy the power to change the fee schedule, should he have done so? Should he have discussed the matter with the city council prior to taking the action? Why or why not?

2. An open democratic society needs a free press, but is it ethical for them to go on a "fishing expedition?"

3. Is the $45 an hour research fee reasonable? Why or why not? Is it ethical to charge such a fee for every request? Carefully read the statute. Does that change your answer? Why or why not? Is it ethical to use such a fee as a deterrent to making such requests? What if the city staff really is overworked, and really does not have the time to fulfill such requests? What ethical theory could be cited to defend the use of such fees as deterrents?

4. This case exemplifies the tension between government transparency and government efficiency. In your opinion, which one of these two values should prevail? Why?

Managing Human Resources

CASE 19: THE PLANNING DIRECTOR AND
THE HR ANALYST

Bill McLaughlin, a Personnel Specialist for the City of Springfield, answered his phone early on a Friday morning. It was the City Manager.

"Bill, we need to fill the Planning Director position. I want you to work with Joseph Ballard on this since he's the Assistant City Manager over planning. He'll be calling you later today to discuss a national search."

"Yes sir." Bill quietly placed the receiver down and began hunting around for his Planning Director file. The position had been vacant for four months. Bill had been curious as to why there was no movement on the position, but assumed that the acting administrator would be moved up without a formal selection process. Obviously not, he thought.

Later that day, Joseph called and Bill went over the desired qualifications of the position and timelines for hiring. Joseph made it clear that he wanted to be involved in all steps of the hiring. That same afternoon, Bill made several calls to planning journals and job listing services to publicize the vacancy announcement. He drew up a draft of the full vacancy announcement and walked it over to Joseph's office for his review. After getting clarification on certain items, he then posted it on the Web site. The Employment Section's Administrative Assistant also put it on the job line. Although the City Manager's Office seemed to be in a hurry to hire, the position was open for almost two months for recruitment in order to ensure a sufficient number of qualified candidates. Periodically over the next several weeks, Bill would review the incoming applications and resumes and report to the Assistant City Manager.

Finally, when the position closed, Bill gathered up all the applications received—sixty-three in all. He compared each one to the desired qualifications and minimum requirements as outlined in the vacancy announcement. After each review, he placed the application and attached resume in one of three piles. The best applications would go in the "In" stack. The obviously unqualified candidates went in the "Out" stack. And close calls went in the

"Maybe" stack. Since Joseph had expressed a desire to be involved, Bill made a call to the secretary at the City Manager's Office to make an appointment. She scheduled a meeting for the following day.

When Bill arrived, he explained about the system of the three stacks. Joseph understood and said, "I would like to review these tonight at home. Let me get back with you tomorrow afternoon and we can discuss who we want to interview for the position."

The next day at the appointed hour, Bill waited patiently outside the Assistant City Manager's office. Eventually he was invited to come in. Joseph had collapsed the applications into two stacks—a very thick one and a very thin one.

"I took a look at these last night, and here are the ones that I suggest that we interview," Joseph said, "As for the other ones, just send them your usual 'thanks, but no thanks' letter and I'll have my secretary call you to schedule the time for the interviews. I would like to get a couple of other people involved, maybe include some people from the community. You know, developers et cetera, who will have to work with whoever we hire."

Bill took the applications back to his office. He discovered to his great relief that Joseph made hardly any changes to his recommendations. Only one application was taken out of the "In" stack and placed in the reject pile. His interest piqued, Bill looked at the application that was removed. The applicant was named Stephanie Grove, the head of planning for another medium-sized city in a nearby state. Bill also noticed that Ms. Grove had previously worked for the City of Springfield. Bill thought this a bit odd that the candidate had been removed from consideration since she was obviously qualified. He thought to himself that maybe it was because she was the only woman to apply. He then thought that the more likely reason was that this woman was a known quantity. In other words, this candidate already had a history with the City which might make her unpalatable to hire back. He went and retrieved her file from the former employee records and found that she had excellent performance evaluations over her previous five-year tenure. "Not everything is reflected on a performance appraisal," he thought to himself, "But who am I to disagree with the Assistant City Manager?" Bill sent Ms. Grove a letter of rejection along with everyone else.

A few days later, he received a telephone call from Ms. Grove. She was livid. She said that she could certainly understand that other candidates might be competitive, but she wanted to know how she was not even being considered for an interview when she had two master's degrees (one in public administration and the other in regional and urban planning) along with four years of very responsible administrative experience, and five years of professional experience with the City of Springfield itself. After all, she was already familiar with Springfield's city operations. She said she knew all the internal candidates and she knew she was at least as qualified as they, and probably more.

Bill of course was at a loss for words. He couldn't come up with any good reasons to rationalize the decision since, if it were his choice, he would have included her in the remainder of the selection process. He also felt a sense of loyalty to the Assistant City Manager so he remained quiet on that issue. Finally, after hearing Ms. Grove have her say, Bill told her that he would take a second look and would call her back.

He immediately called Joseph and explained the situation. Joseph listened, sighed, and then responded, "Go ahead and put her in the selection process. It won't hurt to interview her."

Bill called Stephanie back and said, "Ms. Grove, you're right. We made a mistake and you will be included in the interview process. The interviews will be held next Tuesday. Let me connect you with our secretary to get you scheduled."

After the interviews, Bill tallied up the scores for each candidate. To his surprise, Stephanie was the clear front runner. The next day, the City Manager's Office sent over a justification memo announcing its intention to hire Stephanie Grove. Bill conducted the appropriate background checks and Stephanie was cleared on all fronts. At the end of the week, Joseph called Stephanie and offered her the job. She accepted.

Over the course of the next several months, Bill and the other personnel analysts kept hearing snide comments about the extreme incompetence of the Human Resources Department, especially the Employment Section. Bill certainly understood that since HR was always in a position to tell people "no" more than to tell them "yes," being in the Department was no way to win friends. But these comments were above and beyond the usual grumbling.

Things finally came to a head when the Finance Department made a move to fill the Budget Director position. The Finance Director asked for a meeting with the City Manager to discuss the position and Bill was asked to be in attendance. As Bill came in the room he heard the Finance Director say, "Look, we just can't trust the Human Resources Department to hire for a position this critical. You know what happened with the Planning Director. We just can't afford that kind of sloppiness. Public finance officers in this state are a close-knit group and we all know each other. I am not willing to be professionally embarrassed by our amateur HR Department. I'm saying this in front of Bill because I think it needs to be said."

Bill was almost in shock. He asked, "What do you mean about what happened with the Planning Director?"

The City Manager said, "I've been told by both Joseph and Stephanie how the HR Department botched up the selection process by sending Stephanie a rejection letter and then backtracking. It's particularly embarrassing since she was the one that was ultimately hired. She for one has not let anyone forget it."

DISCUSSION QUESTIONS

1. The Planning Director is a direct executive appointment and the City Manager's office need not have involved the HR Department at all. Should Bill have taken the initiative to ask Joseph about Stephanie's rejection *before* he sent her a letter?

2. Did the HR Department "botch up" the selection process in this case? Was it ethical for Joseph to allow Bill to take all the blame for this situation?

3. Would it be appropriate for Bill to "set the record straight" by giving his side of the story? If Bill should tell his side, how and when should he discuss this situation, and with whom?

4. Perhaps this situation resulted from a "systems problem." How could the selection process be arranged in the future to prevent this situation from occurring again?

CASE 20: PATRONAGE CHARGES AGAINST THE GOVERNOR

Earnest Franklin was elected as the Republican governor. Like most politicians, Franklin had relied heavily upon support from campaign contributions and volunteer workers. Through his campaign Franklin had developed a large grassroots movement, and after his election he sought to pay back as many of his supporters as possible with various appointments in the state government.

Political appointments are common in every state. However, most government employees in every state today are merit employees. Merit employees are not appointed by elected executives, but rather are selected in accordance with objective criteria based on job performance requirements.

Shortly after being elected, Franklin learned that four positions had come open on the State Personnel Board. The State Personnel Board was established during the 1970s as a quasi-judicial body within the state government to hear grievances of state employees.

Any employee subject to the state's Merit Protection Act can file a grievance with the board concerning any employment action taken against them, with the exception of wage and hour decisions.

When an employee files a grievance, his or her case is heard first by an individual member of the board in a quasi-judicial proceeding. The employee is allowed to testify, present evidence, and call witnesses. The agency for which the employee works is also allowed to present testimony and evidence, and to call witnesses. The board member will then consider all the evidence and testimony and issue a report called "Findings of Fact and Conclusions of Law." If neither the employee nor the agency files an appeal, these findings are binding on the employee and the agency. Either party may file an appeal, in which case the record is sent to the entire board for review. The board may then make a determination based on the record alone, or it may grant a new hearing before the entire board which is called a "de novo" review. If either side is unhappy with the decision of the board, it may file an appeal in state court. However, most grievances stop with the decision of the individual board member, especially if the employee prevails after the hearing. The board's enabling statute makes it illegal for any agency, through one or more of its official representatives, to take any adverse action against any employee for filing a grievance with the State Personnel Board. This gives the board a great deal of power regarding the employment conditions of all state merit-protected employees.

Because of the sensitive nature of the claims that the board hears and the need for the appearance of independence, the state legislature decided in its enabling legislation that the board would be a merit-protected agency.

The board is comprised of seven members who are appointed for staggered seven-year terms by the state's Director of Personnel Management on a merit selection basis. All seven members must possess a law degree and be licensed to practice law in the state. Candidates are then given points based on years of experience practicing law, the type of law they practiced, grades in law school, and legal research and writing skills.

When a position on the board comes open, advertisements are placed in all of the state's major newspapers and the state's bar journal inviting the submission of applications. Incumbents are also allowed to re-apply. Once the closing date for the position has passed, three employees from the Office of Personnel Management review the applications based on the criteria and assign point values to each candidate's application. At least two of the employees assigned to the selection process must agree on each candidate's score. The candidates with the top scores are then forwarded to the Director of Personnel Management who is to interview them and, based on the scores, appoint an applicant to the board. Once an applicant has been appointed, he or she cannot be removed from the office prior to the expiration of his or her term except for cause. The only causes for removal from office are defined in the statute and include conditions such as death, incapacitating disability, and felony conviction.

When the Governor learned of the four openings, he contacted Riley Marks, the state's Director of Personnel Management, and asked him to come in for a meeting. Riley is an appointed official of the governor and not covered by the merit protection policy.

Riley arrived at the Governor's office and was quickly ushered into the governor's private office by his personal secretary.

"Good morning Riley." The Governor began. "How are things going for you today?"

"Fine, Governor. What can I do for you today?" Riley replied.

"Well, my Appointments Director noticed that there are four openings in your agency for members of the State Personnel Board. What can you tell me about those positions, Riley?"

"Yes, Governor, there are four openings on the board. The board is appointed by me, but I am bound by statute to use a merit selection process in the appointment. Three merit protected employees review all applications and then forward the top names to me for consideration. I don't have a lot of control over the process," replied Riley.

"The thing is, Riley, I know of four young lawyers who would be good for those jobs. These guys are fresh out of law school and have just passed the state bar. All four worked as volunteers for my campaign, and I know they are dedicated to my conservative philosophy. Plus, they each seem to have that fire in the belly, go get'em dedication. I think they would do just a heck of a job."

"Well, I don't know Governor. One of the areas on which applicants are rated is years of experience practicing law. If these guys are just out of law school, I can't see how they would be competitive. The last Director of Personnel Management told me that when they advertised the positions in the last go round, lawyers with fifteen years of experience in administrative law were applying for the job. It's a fairly high-paying position, and that fact combined with the excellent state benefits makes it a highly sought after job. I just don't think they would even make the cut."

"Look, Riley, if I am going to be effective at implementing my conservative agenda, I need greater control over state agencies. I know these guys' philosophies and they will help me curb the excesses of our out-of-control state employees. This is an important appointment to me. You need to make it happen." The Governor then handed Riley a piece of paper with four names on it.

When Riley left the Governor's office, he was in shock. He didn't know what to do. He knew what the statute said, but he also knew he was a political appointee of the Governor, and he felt like his job was in jeopardy if he didn't find a way to make the appointments happen.

The next day Riley decided that he would find three employees in his agency whom he could trust and confide in them his dilemma. If they were willing to help him out, he would appoint them to the selection committee for the State Personnel Board. This would ensure that the Governor's four names all made the final list and he would be able to appoint the Governor's choices to the board.

Riley was able to find three employees who were willing to help him out, and after the closing date on the position, the employees submitted the names recommended by the Governor along with eight other names to Riley for consideration. Among the eight names not chosen by the Governor were the names of the four incumbents all of whom had been attorneys for over twenty years and had extensive experience in administrative law and procedure.

When Riley received the list, he appointed the four people who had been suggested to him by the Governor. The announcement of the appointments was made in a press release to the state's major newspapers without informing the incumbents prior to its release.

When the incumbent members of the board learned of the decision, they were in shock. One member, Janis Butler, decided to do some investigation on her own. Janis did not recognize any of the names, so she got on the state's bar association Web site and did a members search. To her amazement, all four of the named appointees had just passed the bar during the last year. The new appointees didn't pass the "smell test," and Janis decided that she would contact the state's Attorney General with her concerns.

One of Janis's friends, Lance Haffner, was the First Assistant Attorney General of the Criminal Division. Shortly after learning of the appointments Janis phoned Lance and asked for a meeting and got an appointment for the next day.

At the meeting the next day, Janis began by saying, "Thanks for meeting with me on such short notice. I am not sure where to begin. I don't know if you know it or not, but I have not been re-appointed to my position on the State Personnel Board."

"No. I didn't know that." Lance replied.

"Well, I know it is going to sound like sour grapes, but I just think something is not right. I have served on the board for two terms now, and I have never seen a case where an incumbent who applied did not get re-appointed, and this time it's not just me, but the three other members of the board up for re-appointment didn't get it either."

"That is odd." Lance said. "But do you have some reason to believe that there is something more to it? Do you have some sort of criminal allegation?"

Janis responded, "Well, at first I didn't, but I did some checking on the new appointees. All four of them have just passed the bar exam this last year. Positions on the Board are merit selected and one of the criteria is years of experience practicing law. I know all of the current members each have more than ten years of experience practicing law. This just doesn't pass the smell test. I think the Director bypassed the merit selection process for some reason."

"Well Janis, I can't promise anything, but it certainly sounds suspicious. I will definitely look into this situation."

Based on their conversation, Lance decided to do a little informal checking on his own. He easily found State Ethics Commission reports for Governor Franklin that listed "in-kind donations of personal service" by the four new appointees to the State Personnel Board. With this information, Lance went to see his boss, Attorney General Arthur "Art" Danker.

Art had been elected Attorney General as a Democrat in 1998, and had been at odds with the Republican Governor over a number of issues.

Lance began his meeting with the Attorney General by saying, "Art, I believe that Governor Franklin may have committed malfeasance in office."

"Why would you think that?" said Art.

"Well, I was made aware of some unusual appointments to the State Personnel Board. It seems that some seemingly unqualified applicants were appointed, and that those same individuals had donated their time to help the election of Governor Franklin. It seems just a little too coincidental."

"That does seem odd. You can investigate, but before anything becomes public about this, you had better be damn sure you're right. Got it?"

With Art's permission to proceed, Lance decided to interview the Director of Personnel Management, Riley Marks. Riley turned out to be extremely soft. The minute Lance walked into Riley's office and told him why he was there, Riley admitted that the Governor had pressured him to violate the merit protection laws and appoint his chosen people. Lance even got Riley to sign a confession after reading Riley his Miranda Rights.

Lance then made an appointment to interview the Governor. At the meeting, Lance told the Governor why he was there, and that he had a signed confession from Riley. At that point, the Governor said, "I have no comment, and this meeting is over."

Based on Riley's confession, Lance convinced Art to seek a grand jury hearing. The district court granted the request and a grand jury was impaneled for the following month.

Governor Franklin instantly went on the defensive, and granted blanket pardons to Riley and the four appointees, hoping to stop them from talking. This tactic was somewhat effective; however, the Attorney General still had Riley's sworn statement. As a result, an agreement was reached by the Attorney General and the Governor, and approved by the court. The Governor's appointees would resign, the Governor would admit that there were some improprieties; however, he would not be charged with any crime. The outcome resulted largely from the difficulty of prosecuting the case based on one statement made by an appointee of the Governor who was now free to refuse to testify in person because of the blanket pardon he had received.

DISCUSSION QUESTIONS

1. Did Riley act in an ethical fashion? What theories and arguments can be made that he did? What facts would support such an argument? What theories and arguments can be made that he didn't act ethically?
2. Should the governor have more control over state agencies to implement his or her agenda? People elect a governor to carry out policies that he or she promises during their campaign. However, governors are often then constrained by merit protection systems which allow state employees more freedom to resist a governor's policies. Is this ethical or even desirable? Why or why not?
3. If Janis acted purely out of self-interest, did she act ethically? Why or why not? Was it ethical for her to consult her friend at the Office of Attorney General, or should she have simply filed a report with the first available assistant attorney general? Was it ethical of Lance to investigate a claim in which a personal friend had an interest?
4. Since the Attorney General is of a different party than the Governor, and since he has clashed with the Governor in the past, should he have requested an "independent counsel" in this case? Why or why not? Was the "plea bargain" between the Governor and the Attorney General ethical? What theories can be used to justify plea bargains? What theory can be used to oppose such agreements?

CASE 21: SELECTING THE SPECIAL ASSISTANT TO THE CITY COUNCIL

The long-time special assistant to the city council had retired. Assistant City Manager Beth Grace called Ron Shoemake, the city's Employment Manager and delivered the message, "The city manager says that you'll need to perform a full-blown selection process, including an assessment center."

"That's a bit of an overkill for what's basically an advanced clerical position," said Ron. "Besides, it's not technically under the union contract—so why all the fuss since the mayor and council can basically hire anyone they like?"

"You know they can't agree on anything, so the mayor and city manager decided to make sure there is no whiff of politics on this one."

"Okay, my staff and I will get right on this, but I hope the city manager realizes this will be expensive." Ron hung up the phone and called in Alice Wren, the Lead Personnel Analyst.

"Alice, I need you to prepare a register of eligible candidates for the special assistant to the city council. We'll need to do a complete selection process, including an assessment center."

Alice looked surprised. "I hope they're not expecting to hire quickly."

"We'll have to do our best, so you better get on this one. Get the announcement posted this morning on the internals. We're not going outside. Then, go ahead and get a written test prepared and see if we have any assessment center projects on similar positions we can adapt for this one."

The following week, Alice reported to Ron, "We'll be administering the written test for the next couple of days and the assessment center is ready. There are twenty-four candidates testing and we'll take the top twelve to advance to the assessment center."

"So what's in store for the lucky twelve?"

"We're doing an in-basket exercise, a role play with a difficult citizen, and a letter-writing scenario."

"Sounds good," Ron said. "Keep me informed."

Three days later, Alice handed Ron the score sheet for the special assistant selection process:

Name	Test	Assess	Composite
1. Tammy Carlson	89	90	89.5
2. Janet Langley	91	87	89.0
3. Patrick North	84	91	87.5
4. Anna Farley	90	84	87.0
5. Corinna Beeson	82	87	84.5
6. Melody Gordon	88	81	84.5
7. Julie Hankins	86	82	84.0
8. Jack Whisenhunt	87	81	84.0
9. Melanie Harrison	83	85	84.0
10. Jane Princeton	86	82	84.0
11. Karla Morrison	81	78	79.5
12. Carrie Marker	78	76	77.0

"Interesting," Ron said as he glanced down through the list. "That should give them something to gnaw on. So, how many are you going to send forward?"

"Well, if this position was covered by the union contract, we would have to send at least the top five. I'm going to recommend to Beth that we have them interview the top ten. As you can tell there's a tie between Beeson and Gordon for fifth place. And then there's only a half point difference between their scores and the next four. Then we have a significant score break between Princeton and Morrison."

"Inform Beth and then schedule the interviews."

Alice left Ron's office but quickly returned with Beth.

"Look who I found lurking in our lobby waiting for the results," Alice said as she motioned Beth into Ron's office. Alice handed Beth the score sheet and said, "We're recommending that the council interview the top ten."

Beth scanned the list and then said, "I think we'd like to interview all twelve."

Alice looked to Ron. Ron said, "I'm not comfortable with that. Our standard operating procedure for positions at this level is to send the top five except when you have a tight cluster of scores which we do in this case. But that cluster ends at ten."

Beth said, "I'll take the heat. I think we should give the council as much choice as possible." She then left without waiting for a response.

"What was that all about?" asked Ron.

"I don't know . . . ," Alice replied. "But I think you should know that when I set up the assessment center, I originally recommended only the top ten and Beth asked me to see if we could get Carrie Marker in as well. I didn't see any harm in including her."

"She speaks for the city manager, so go ahead and let them interview all twelve. We'll see what happens."

At the end of the week, Beth appeared in Ron's doorway and said, "The council has made its selection."

"Let me call in Alice, since she's managed this process." Ron took his phone and called in Alice. In the meantime, Beth handed Ron the name. Sure enough, it was Carrie Marker.

When Alice arrived, Ron informed her of the proposed selection. Alice started to object, but Ron interrupted her and said to Beth, "Look, we certainly understand that in making hiring and promotion decisions, managers need and deserve a lot of discretion, but I have to tell you this is raising several red flags."

"Ron, this decision is made. I don't really want to debate it. I just want you to complete the paperwork. I've already informed Carrie that she's being promoted."

"Whoa! Beth, you're jumping the gun on this. Let me explain," Ron searched for the words. "Even though it's not covered by the union contract, we have a selection process here for a classified position. At the top of the list, you have Tammy Carlson who is an African American female over forty. You also have Patrick North, a veteran with a war disability who is also over forty. In fact, this list is sprinkled with applicants belonging to various protected classes. Melody Gordon is pregnant. You also have an Asian and two Hispanics. At the bottom of the list is one who in my judgment we shouldn't have forwarded on to the next step in the first place. Carrie is white and in her mid-twenties. These are prima facie violations of Title VII of the 1964 Civil Rights Act, the Age Discrimination in Employment Act, Americans with Disabilities Act, and several other federal and state laws. Regardless of race and ethnicity and disability and all that, you are wanting to hire the person whom an extremely valid, multi-hurdle selection process says is the least qualified. Carrie even has the least seniority. You don't want to tempt the union to fight us over this. Most important, the city won't be able to withstand any kind of legal challenge. You need to think about this."

"Thinking is over, Ron. Carrie has been offered the job and she's accepted. Politics are going on here way above our pay grades. I just need you to sign this buckslip so that HRIS will get the changes made in the computer."

DISCUSSION QUESTIONS

1. The special assistant to the city council has obviously been exempted from the union contract and other normal hiring procedures because of its inherent political nature. Was it therefore inappropriate to allow a full-blown competitive hiring process to be conducted for this position in the first place? Why or why not?
2. To protect the privacy of applicants, specific information about much of the hiring process must remain confidential. Would Ron be justified in "leaking" this information to any of the candidates—or, at least suggesting that they file a grievance to investigate this further? Or, does his professional role in city management mean that he has a higher duty to maintain confidentiality as well as to protect the city from possible legal challenges?
3. Should Ron sign the buckslip? What are the possible ramifications if he does so? What are the possible ramifications if he refuses?
4. Is Beth well representing the interests of the city manager? Why or why not?

CASE 22: MAINTAINING PAY DURING REDUCTION IN FORCE

"Mr. Norris. The budget office wants to reschedule your 9:30 meeting with them until 10:00 if that's all right. Also, Leon and Richard from Human Resources are here to see you, if you have a moment," said the city manager's secretary. She waited for a response while he finished typing on his computer.

"Fine, send them in." The budget for the next fiscal year was shaping up to be a major challenge and Jack Norris knew that he was going to be working long hours until the financial crisis was under control.

Leon, the Compensation Manager for the city, came into the city manager's office first followed closely by Richard, the Employment Manager. Leon broke the silence.

"Jack, thanks for seeing us on such short notice. Richard and I have been talking this morning about the reduction in force that's about to hit the city. Almost every department will be sacrificing several positions. Richard tells me that in spite of that, there are enough vacant positions to cover probably every employee affected."

"Could you explain that?" Mr. Norris said.

"If I may, Mr. Norris," interjected Richard. "You see in every budget cycle we have departments that delete or add positions in the new fiscal year. Those employees come to my office for career counseling and placement services. The city managers in the past have always supported us in making sure that current city employees don't actually lose their jobs if they are qualified for vacant positions in the city. Sometimes we get lucky and we are able to lateral those affected employees into equivalent positions. The problem is that usually these positions are demotions for the employees involved. Yesterday, my staff and I spent several hours looking over the new budget plans submitted by the departments. Even though we're cutting dozens of positions citywide and not adding any new ones, there are enough vacant positions currently so that every one who shows up to work on the first day of the fiscal year will still have a job. Except for a handful, these will be demotions. What we've counted so far are twenty-four employees whose current positions with the city will disappear in the new fiscal year."

Leon jumped back in the conversation, "Those deletions are what balances the budget for next fiscal year. But we'll still have over two dozen vacancies that remain in the budget."

"Okay, I get it," said Mr. Norris. "Instead of these folks losing their jobs outright, they can take a demotion."

"Right," said Richard, "but that still leaves a big problem. One of the principles of human resources management is that you don't cut someone's pay. That makes them disgruntled and bitter. It demotivates them. When asked to do something they drag their feet. They won't take the initiative. They drive down morale. They're even known to engage in sabotage. It sounds cold-hearted, but it's really better just to let them go than to let them hang around with bad feelings festering and infecting the rest of the workforce."

"You're recommending then, that we let these employees go?"

"Quite the contrary," said Leon. "Let the employment staff place these folks in existing vacant positions with one condition: In terms of salary, keep these employees whole."

"What do you mean?" asked Mr. Norris.

"They get demoted," said Richard, "but they get to keep their current salaries."

"That doesn't make sense," said Mr. Norris. "We won't generate any savings from payroll."

"You would think," said Leon. "I know it's counterintuitive . . . the savings comes from deleting the positions. I've done the math, and I'm here to tell you that the difference between demoting these employees and keeping their salaries the same is only about $12,000. It's a drop in the bucket; it's not even one full-time equivalent."

"Let me think this through." Mr. Norris closed his eyes for a few seconds. "I foresee a different problem with this scenario. You're going to have employees working side by side with the same job title and same job duties, but with possibly very different pay. That'll cause a morale problem right there."

"We've thought of that," said Richard, "and you're right, it might be a problem in a few situations. On the other hand, it shows to all employees—even those unaffected by this year's RIF—that the city is going to take care of them, even in an economic downturn. People will understand because they know that they might be in a similar situation in the future. I think if we present this well and frame it right, our employees will understand. It's going to be hard on a lot of people—there's no minimizing that—and of course, most people aren't going to be thrilled with a demotion, even with keeping their current pay, but it's an extremely significant gesture."

Leon said, "The other complication is that these RIF'd employees are going to be outside the pay range for the positions they occupy. In practical terms, that means that they won't be getting any pay raises until cost-of-living increases bring the entire pay scale up to the level of their frozen salaries."

"The good news there," said Richard, "is that they will have an incentive to get promoted to higher positions when they get the opportunity."

"The budget staff will be coming here in a few minutes," said Mr. Norris. "I'll talk it over with them and get back with you. I don't know if we'll do it, but it's worth thinking about. Thanks, guys!"

DISCUSSION QUESTIONS

1. Overall, will this solution be more likely to raise or reduce employee morale? Explain.
2. Is the proposed solution geared more for taking care of employees in the short term or the long term? Why?
3. What other possible consequences of this action can you foresee? What about equal pay for equal work?
4. Should public opinion play a role in adopting this proposal? Should the city council be consulted? How do you think the public will react to the city manager if he approves this decision?

CASE 23: A SPEED BUMP ON STAFF

Penny Perkins, Director of the state agency for Child Support Enforcement, strode joyfully into the office on a cold Monday morning. She was very excited, and dropped her double mocha latte as she rifled through her purse for her keys. Debbie Schnebel, her Administrative Assistant, jumped up to help, unlocking her boss's office door. Penny told Debbie to leave the spill for later and "get everyone together immediately for an important meeting in the conference room." Ten minutes later, Penny was distributing copies of a diagram to her sixteen subordinates seated around the table. The diagram depicted three different grades of employees—the top 20 percent (the "stars"), the middle 60 percent (the "spear carriers"), and the bottom 20 percent (the "drags")—each corresponding to a different compensation strategy.

"I wanted to share with you all a new management approach. It's from a book I just read called *The Compensation Solution* by John E. Tropman. Tropman's main idea is that the compensation system holds a lot of potential as a lever we can pull to get the most from our human resources. He really thinks of employees in the most positive ways, and he wants to give them the best chance to enhance their rewards by enhancing their performance. I think he has a lot of good ideas that could improve the performance of our agency, and we all know how weak the connection is between performance and reward around here. Anyway, please take a moment to look over the diagram while I go clean up a coffee spill."

After a minute or two, Abner Corum was the first to speak. "I like it," he said aloud to no one in particular.

"Of course you like it," Bob Traywick retorted. "What a brown-noser! To me it looks like some of us are on the way out. Which ones of us are the 'organizational drags' who will be encouraged to leave by being paid '10 to 20 percent below market'?"

Just then Penny returned. "Don't worry Bob," she said. "You are a 'star' in my book. That means you should be getting 10 to 20 percent above market. So, what do the rest of us think about these three categories of employees—'stars,' 'spear carriers,' and 'drags'?"

Carly Lawrence said, "I think the 'spear carrier' label sounds racist. Other than that, I know there is some validity in Tropman's categories. I agree that most employees are in that middle category, and they should be paid a market-based wage. And the 'stars' like Bob ought to get more. By the way, I'm a star too. But seriously, we all know we'd be in a real bind if Bob left for another agency, or the private sector."

"OK," said Penny. "What do you think, Ruth?" Ruth Newbold paused to carefully consider her reply. She and Penny had been rivals for the Director's position that ultimately went to Penny.

"I've got to be honest on this matter, Penny. I think it's a good idea— especially getting rid of the 'drags'—but one that will never be implemented at this agency. Maybe it can't be done because of civil service rules, or human resources policy, or whatever. I just don't see it happening. But I do agree with the principle of emulating the private sector more than we do—especially when it comes to the role of compensation as a motivational tool." Penny was happily surprised to hear Ruth's expression of support for the ideas. If Ruth is on board, she thought, a major obstacle is removed. But then Debbie, clearing her throat audibly, raised her hand as if to request permission to speak.

"Yes, Debbie," said Penny cheerfully. "What do you think?"

"Well, I just wanted to let everyone know that all of us administrative assistants just went through our four-day training on HR procedures. It was really very helpful, because it made us think very consciously about all the different techniques managers are using to get around our policies and procedures. This plan looks like it goes against every principle we've ever followed. I can't help wondering how we will do performance evaluations, what will happen to our classification system, and if this will be perceived as unfair. How can it be motivational to say that only one employee in five is a star, while everyone else is a spear carrier or a drag?"

"Well those are good points to consider, Debbie," said Penny. "Anything else?"

"Well, maybe just one other thing. It seems you are all open to trying this out, and maybe that's okay. But who is going to do all the dirty work? I guess it will end up being me."

"I don't understand," Penny replied. "What sort of dirty work do you mean?"

"Well," said Debbie, "the way it is now, I facilitate employee-manager relations more or less single-handedly. Penny, when you need to evaluate employees, I gather the information you need regarding performance expectations. And Bob, when you are up for review, I help you put your packet in order. So I'm the one who helps both sides come out okay. That works fine for now, because the performance evaluation doesn't really impact anything within the unit, certainly not anyone's pay. We do performance evaluation to protect our unit from attacks by the executive team and other units."

Debbie paused and noticed everyone staring at her. They were surprised to hear Debbie go on at such length, because she usually had very little to say. But everyone remained attentive, so she continued, "What kind of position will I be in when we are trying to identify some drags, and cut their pay so that we can free up money to pay more to the stars? People who don't look good on paper are going to blame me, because I track everyone's numbers. And if Penny wants to get rid of someone, I could feel pressure to facilitate that outcome. Then again, when someone comes out looking like a star, my work will be scrutinized by everyone else who doesn't. I really don't want to be put in an awkward position like that, and I don't think it's fair to put that kind of burden on my shoulders. I'm not paid enough for that."

DISCUSSION QUESTIONS

1. Describe in general terms the culture of public agencies with respect to human resource management. Are the challenges outlined by Debbie rooted in organizational culture (public and private sector), in public sector culture exclusively, or in the specific characteristics of her position in that particular agency? What would it take to effectively deal with Debbie's concerns? How long would it take?

2. Evaluate the potential for increased organizational performance stemming from changes in the compensation system. List at least three assumptions underlying Tropman's main idea. Are these assumptions reasonable? How valuable is performance appraisal in the compensation process? What other managerial objectives does performance appraisal serve? Are these objectives sometimes at cross-purposes?

3. Consider Ruth's ambivalence toward the plan. What strategies could be used to loosen the grip of civil service rules and regulations? Should civil service rules and regulations be loosened? Why or why not?

4. Does implementation of performance pay in the public sector face unique challenges not seen in the private sector? If so, describe these challenges.

CASE 24: THE BUREAUCRAT'S WIFE

Clair Wolff had been through this before. Being the wife of one of the nation's most high-profile bureaucrats certainly has its moments, but for Clair the old adage about taking the bad with the good was ringing more true with each passing day. Her husband, "Abe" Wolff, was engaged in yet another extra-marital affair. This time, however, Abe's wayward adventures endangered not only their marriage, but also Abe's candidacy for the top post at the Central Intelligence Agency (CIA), and perhaps even the foreign policy goals of the incoming U.S. President. In other words, this was a serious matter—serious enough that the president's loyal Vice President-elect decided to handle the matter personally.

Always the ultimate "Beltway" insider, the Vice President-elect felt confident he could orchestrate a solution. He immediately placed a call to the Lexington School at Hampshire University, where Abe was serving as Dean of the Graduate Program in International Affairs. Abe picked up right away.

"Congratulations Mr. Vice President," he bubbled. "So great to hear from you! How is the transition going?"

"Oh, I guess we're settling in, Abe. As you know, it's like being in crazy town here, with everyone angling for position. The President is hoping to get a 'yes' from Calvin Powers today or tomorrow. With the General heading up the State Department, we definitely need to balance that out with the CIA post. General Powers is a slam-dunk politically, but he is not onboard ideologically. As our intelligence chief, you'll be able to neutralize his influence. That's going to be very important as we execute our Middle East policy."

"Well, of course, it is so very humbling to hear you say that," Abe replied. "I stand ready to serve the President however he sees fit. Is there anything I should be doing right now?"

"Actually, there is one thing, Abe. See if you can calm down that wife of yours. She wrote a letter to the President saying you should be considered a national security risk. We both know what she's talking about, Abe, but the good news is my assistant Alec Bozarth intercepted the letter. The President hasn't seen it, and he never will. Let's hope she doesn't involve the press. We need to focus on damage control so we can get you in position."

"I see," Abe replied. "I guess you haven't heard that Clair and I are separated. I should also tell you that her attorney is pretty aggressive, so things may get worse before they get better. But I must say, the idea that I pose a security risk is hogwash. My foreign policy credentials are unquestioned, as is my loyalty. I'm sure you and the President both remember my work on the strategy committee. It would be a travesty for this personal matter to take precedence."

"Of course I agree with you Abe. The thing is, Clair's letter has one point that gives me pause. As you remember, none of us cared when you were seen around town with Jillian. But you must admit that your new girlfriend is more problematic. Do you know what I'm referring to?"

"You mean the fact that she's Muslim."

"Yes."

"I see. Do you have any suggestions as to what I should do?"

"Well, Abe, of course the best case scenario is to break it off. Otherwise we'll end up having to explain this at the confirmation hearings and in the press."

"That's funny, because this woman is well known as a staunch supporter of our plan for the Middle East. Her scholarly record is squarely aligned with us on every point."

"You are right about that, I know. But so often the nuances of a situation get lost in the process. People like us understand, but the American public may not get it. And our opponents would salivate over this. We just don't want things like this getting in the way."

"OK," said Abe. "I'll end the relationship. The truth is, my attorney gave me the same advice. I hope you will assure the President that he will have nothing to worry about with my nomination."

DISCUSSION QUESTIONS

1. Thinking about Clair's letter, what ethical framework might have influenced her behavior? Does Clair have a conflict of interest? Could she be correct that Abe's behavior constitutes a potential risk to national security? Suppose Abe were to do some soul searching about his personal behavior and career aspirations. What ethical guidance would you give him?

2. According to Weber's description of bureaucracy, a public official keeps his or her personal life separate from his or her professional obligations. Does this imply that Abe's personal life ought to be off limits at the confirmation hearing? What factors are relevant to Abe's fitness for the position?

3. Consider the situation in the context of Wilson's politics-administration dichotomy. Do high-level appointees act more in the role of administrators or politicians?

4. From an organizational perspective, evaluate the Vice President-elect's decision to have Bozarth intercept the letter. Do you think the situation has been managed effectively?

Public Health and Welfare

CASE 25: PENNIES FROM HEAVEN

Patrick Ulmer was the new Director of the state Department of Health and Human Services (DHHS). He had been recruited from out of state, and had come on an early morning flight to meet with the Governor and the other cabinet members. They seemed pleasant enough, but many hinted that the department he was taking over had a lot of problems. He went over to his new building and wandered around the halls for a bit. Patrick's appointment had not yet been made official, so he thought it prudent to keep a low profile. He noticed that no one seemed to pay any attention to him even as he walked through areas where he should have been treated as a customer. Even worse, he noticed that he was ignored even when he walked into areas where it was clear that the presence of an unauthorized individual might compromise client confidentiality.

Lunchtime approached, so he made his way to the office canteen to get something to eat. He sat by himself in the corner and observed the people around him. He realized that he would shortly be supervising many of them. A young man sat down in the booth next to his. Patrick could read from his name tag that he was a "Social Services Field Officer" named Henry Walsh.

Henry's cell phone sounded and he began conversing in a loud tone of voice with the person on the other end. Patrick was then treated to a loud one-way conversation.

"Yeah, a similar thing happened to me the other day," he heard Henry say. "There was this old lady. She won a thousand, maybe fifteen hundred dollars playing bingo. And, of course, I realized she's going to have to do a 'spend down' and I'd have to do a bunch of paperwork. She was going to use that money to pay her bills. I said, 'I won't say anything if you don't. Congrats!'" Henry laughed heartily at his own comment and then continued, "Then a message came up on my error screen from the IRS and I deleted that baby like crazy! Well, you know . . . that lady was making seven hundred something dollars per month. I mean she was literally barely, barely scraping by.

You know damn well she didn't have enough resources or she couldn't have been on the program in the first place. Well, she probably never had pennies from heaven like that in her whole life. You know. I told her to go spend it. That's what she would have had to do anyway. I told her that when you do a 'spend down' all you have to do is come up with whatever you spent it on. Well, I mean . . . *technically* . . . I should have put it in and she would have lost her benefits for two or three months. If I ever get dragged into court on it, I guess I'd have to admit I did it . . . probably even though it'd cost me my damn job. Because, you know, I know what policy is, but it would have cost more man-hours. You see, you do something like that, the man-hour costs are incredible. And we would have had to shut her off for a long period of time. When you do that, you bump up against social security and all that. . . on and on and on. Well, that's nuts. She would have spent the money anyway. Okay, I'll talk at you later. Just remember, I for one think you did the right thing too, so don't sweat it."

Patrick left the canteen for his flight back to get his wife and family ready for the move. He would have two more weeks before taking over. He realized that he had a lot to think about between now and then.

DISCUSSION QUESTIONS

1. Was it ethical for Henry to allow the woman to keep her gambling proceeds? Why or why not?
2. Should Henry have been advising his coworker to do the same thing? Why or why not?
3. Does Patrick have an ethical obligation to report what he heard to someone at the department? Even if he does *not* take the job? If Patrick does take the job, does he have an obligation to take some action with regard to Henry?
4. Should administrators have discretion in situations like the one above, or should they always follow the rules? What would a utilitarian ethicist say about following the rules and why? What would a Kantian ethicist say about the rules?

CASE 26: SPANKING THE FOSTER CHILD

Jennifer was new to her job as a Child Welfare Protection Specialist. As a trainee, she had been assigned to follow Daryl, a more senior Specialist on his rounds. As she sat reading standard operating procedures, her telephone rang. It was Daryl.

"C'mon. We just got an assignment," Daryl said. "Meet me downstairs and I'll give you directions. I thought we could take our own cars since it's so late in the day."

Jennifer turned off her computer, gathered her things, and ran downstairs. Daryl was already waiting in the lobby.

"Here's the address. It's a rural route so I drew you a map. It's about ten minutes west of town."

"I think I know where this is," Jenny responded. "What's this all about?"

"We got a tip that there might be a problem with some foster children. Let me call you on the cell phone with the details. We need to hurry, because we'll be working overtime as it is."

Jennifer got in her car. She decided to try to follow Daryl if she could so she wouldn't get lost. She spotted him on the road already, but through some skillful maneuvering she was able to get her car behind his. As they sat at the traffic light, she could see Daryl pick up his cell phone. Within seconds, her phone sounded.

"Hello."

"Hi. Okay, let me tell you what's going on," Daryl began. "This morning we got a call from Jason Halworth who's a 14-year-old ward of the state. His father is unknown and his mother's in drug rehab. I'm familiar with Jason's case. Basically, he's been in and out of trouble for the past several years. You know, drugs, your basic hooliganism, and all that. Nothing violent . . . yet. Anyway, he and his 10-year-old brother and 6-year-old sister are staying with Charles and Jane Caravan."

"Who are they?" asked Jennifer.

"They're a very nice couple who've served as foster parents for dozens of kids over the past several years," Daryl said. "They've got a good reputation and we've given them some of our toughest kids. I would include Jason as one of those."

"But you said he's the one who made the call."

"Yeah, he says that Charlie Caravan spanked his little brother."

"Oh, I see. And of course that's not allowed."

"Right. As you may have read in the SOPs, foster parents are strictly forbidden to physically strike any of the children. They've received training and, of course, they have to sign a statement that they understand the rules. Hold on, I'm going to pass this truck ahead of me. If we get separated, just turn left at the next intersection. It's about a mile ahead."

Daryl passed the slow moving truck and Jennifer followed soon after.

"Sorry," Daryl continued. "I can't drive and talk at the same time. Where was I?"

"You said that Mr. Caravan spanked the little boy."

"At least that's what Jason says. We're just going to do an initial investigation and get everyone's story. We'll then take it to the County Judge. We may have to do it tonight if it's serious enough. All right . . . turn left here."

After driving a bit longer, the two cars turned into a long unpaved driveway that led to what looked like an old farm house. They parked outside near the fence line. As they got out, Charles Caravan stepped out his front door and off his front porch.

"Hey, Daryl! What brings you guys out here?"

"It's just routine Charlie. We have an issue we need to make a report on."

"Haven't seen you for a while," Charles said, "and I don't believe I've had the pleasure of meeting the young lady."

"This is Jennifer Warren. She's new to the department. She's been tagging along with me to learn the ropes."

After exchanging pleasantries, Charles invited them both in the house. Even though the living room was dimly lit, Jennifer could see pictures of the "Caravan children" all around the room. Jane Caravan came out of the kitchen looking a bit flustered.

"Oh, Charlie, I didn't realize we had guests."

"Yep. Daryl's here from Child Welfare and this is Jennifer."

"Nice to meet you, Jennifer," Jane said, "Would either of you like some coffee or tea?"

"I think we both could use some water if you don't mind," Daryl said for them both.

"What can we do for you today?" Charles asked.

"We got a phone call this morning from Jason. He says that you spanked little Tommy. Is that true?"

Charles looked startled. "Uh, yeah . . . but I have to tell you it was an extraordinary situation."

Daryl remained silent. Charles continued. "I was in the kitchen and I noticed that Beth had climbed up in that old mimosa tree out there. That wood is soft and those branches break quite easily. I thought it was a bit dangerous for her so I was going to go outside and get her down. When I stepped out into the front yard, I saw little Tommy was standing just below her, throwing rocks at her. I thought if one connected, she'd get knocked plum out of the tree. I panicked. I ran like heck, screaming the whole way. He kept on throwin' those stones. When I got there, I put him on my knee and gave him a couple of whacks on his behind. I thought he was going to kill his sister. I guess he didn't know what he was doing, but I needed him to learn. I realized that it broke policy, but you know, at the time I wasn't thinking about that."

"I understand," Daryl said. "I'll need to get a statement from the kids as well."

"Sure, uh, Tommy and Beth are in the back there. I'll go find Jason."

"Thanks," Daryl said as he went to the back bedrooms. He motioned for Jennifer to follow. After talking with all three children, Daryl whispered to Jane that it was time to leave.

"Mrs. Caravan, once again, thank you for your hospitality," Daryl said. He led Jennifer back to their cars. The sun was just setting. Daryl waited until the Caravans and the Halworth children went back into the house.

Jennifer turned to Daryl and asked, "What are we going to do?"

"There's only one thing we can do. I'll make a call to the judge when we get back into town. I expect he'll need one of us back out here this evening to accompany the sheriff when the children are pulled out."

"You've got to be kidding!" Jennifer was flabbergasted. "Didn't you see those pictures on the wall and those notes from former foster kids everywhere? I can tell that the Caravans love those children, and I mean the Halworth kids, too."

"I agree. It's hard, but policy is very clear on this issue—no exceptions. The Halworths have to know what's going to happen. They've been part of the system for quite some time."

"But little Beth and Tommy—I think they're happy here. I can't say for Jason, but I believe the Caravans are really helping the younger kids. After all, they've been through so much."

"I'll talk it over with the judge, but my recommendation is that we take them out of the house immediately." Jason opened his car door. "I'll call you tonight if we need you. Otherwise, I'll see you tomorrow."

DISCUSSION QUESTIONS

1. Is corporal punishment ever necessary? Is it ethical? Even if it is ethical, are there better methods of discipline? Justify your answer.
2. Should Daryl make an exception in this case and not file a report? To what extent should a case worker have discretion to grant exceptions to the rules? Would it be ethical to overlook what happened, just this once?
3. If Daryl does file a report with the County Court, what should the judge do? Should the judge decide not to follow the policy in this case? Should he or she have that power? Why? Should judges strictly apply a statute, or should they do what they think is right? What if a statute or regulation is unclear? If the judge does strictly follow the regulation in this case, has "justice" been done?
4. Was it ethical for Daryl and Jennifer to talk on their cell phones while driving? Why or why not? What about using their personal vehicles for official business?

CASE 27: CHILDREN ABUSED IN STATE INSTITUTION

Readers of the *Capitol Observer* were shocked, one late January morning, to read the front page headlines, "Children Abused in State Institution." The story alleged that children with severe developmental and mental disabilities were being subjected to cruel conditions, including outright physical abuse by direct care workers, in the Hillmark Evaluation Center. The article quoted Jonathan Freeman, an ex-employee, who charged that children unable to take care of themselves were frequently left unattended, with some forced to sit or lie in soiled diapers for hours. Freeman further claimed that since attendants were afraid to discipline children for fear of getting into trouble, they had begun to rely on other residents to "punish" problem children. According to the story, direct care workers would encourage older residents to "tease" the younger residents, which was a euphemism for physical abuse.

Derrick Sheffield, Deputy Director of Health and Human Services, held a press conference that afternoon to discuss the allegations. Derrick read an opening statement:

> I've called this press conference today to discuss the allegations printed in the morning edition of the *Capitol Observer*. As many of you are aware, we have had trouble in the past with the Hillmark Evaluation Center, and it's scheduled to close at the end of the year, by court order. It is true that two attendants were found to be encouraging physical abuse among the residents, but both were terminated earlier this month . . . well before the story in the *Observer*. We have had great difficulty in

attracting quality people to Hillmark precisely because we can't promise them permanent employment after closure of the facility. Currently, we have sixty-three children whom we are treating and housing at Hillmark. Health and Human Services remains committed to providing these children the best care possible, but irresponsible statements as made by a disgruntled employee and prominently displayed in the state's largest newspaper do nothing to help the situation. I am announcing today the formation of a task force of policy leaders and health professionals to seek immediate improvement. We still have eleven months before the facility is scheduled to close and these children are sent to private group homes. In the meantime, we must remain vigilant in ensuring the highest quality of care possible. Thank you.

Derrick took several questions from reporters, answering most by saying, "I'm sure the task force will look into it." The task force gathered later that week to discuss the problems at Hillmark. Forty-four staff members remained at Hillmark with an additional twenty-seven part-time temporary workers hired to help handle the patient load of sixty-three on a 24-hour basis. Talk among task force members included the dismissal of all facility employees and accelerated contracting out of services.

DISCUSSION QUESTIONS

1. How well did Derrick handle the public relations aspect of this predicament? Is keeping the press at bay a normal function of high-level bureaucratic positions? How far should a public administrator go to help the press do its job? Are there limits?
2. Is it appropriate to handle an allegation of child abuse by creating a task force to solve the problem? Can such a task force be more than a symbolic gesture? If you were a member on this task force, how would you approach your duties? Are there better alternatives to a task force? If so, list and explain.
3. What are the advantages and disadvantages to having a private company treat and house children with mental and developmental disabilities? Can a private company be held as accountable as a public agency? What controls would you recommend to maintain quality standards, whether these kinds of services are conducted by a private or a public organization? Are there differences between the two? Would a nonprofit agency be a viable institutional setting to manage services for children with severe developmental and mental disabilities?
4. Evaluate the effectiveness of using part-time temporary workers to fill in the gaps as experienced full-time employees find jobs in other facilities. How could you best manage this kind of situation to ease the transition?

CASE 28: SMOKING AT THE STATE HEALTH DEPARTMENT

Dr. Paul Billingsley was recently hired from out of state to head the Department of Health and Human Services. After a few days on the job, Dr. Billingsley noticed that a large number of the department's workers were smokers and that the smokers seemed to spend a lot of time going outside to take smoke breaks.

The department's mission statement read in part, "To promote the overall health and well-being of the citizens of the state by providing necessary medical, fitness, and mental health programs and services."

Dr. Billingsley felt that the number of smokers in the department did a disservice to the citizens and did not project the right image for a Department of Health and Human Services. So, after three months on the job, Dr. Billingsley issued a memorandum and policy update to all members of the department that read in part, "Beginning immediately, there will be no smoking on department grounds. Further, all employees are hereby notified that six months from the date of this memorandum the department will test all employees for nicotine. Any employee who tests positive will be given six months to quit smoking or be terminated. The department will compensate employees for participation in any type of smoking cessation program they wish to use to accomplish this goal."

The new policy sent a shock wave through the department. Employees who smoked formed a group to protest the new policy. The workers initially sent a letter, signed by every employee who smoked, requesting that Dr. Billingsley retract the new policy. The letter stated that they did not object to the portion of the policy that prohibited smoking on state property, but that what they did on their own time should be no concern of Dr. Billingsley.

Dr. Billingsley replied that he would not change the policy, and that any further protest by employees would be considered insubordination and would be grounds for termination. As a result, the employees began to write letters to their state legislators protesting the new policy and asking that the legislature intervene in this matter.

A number of legislators did take up the issue and decided to hold hearings. When Dr. Billingsley was called to testify before both a house and senate committee on the issue, he demanded to know which employees had written letters. All the legislators who received letters declined to provide Dr. Billingsley with the names of any employee who wrote a letter.

DISCUSSION QUESTIONS

1. What do you think of Dr. Billingsley's policy? Is this policy ethical? Why or why not? Justify your answer. What would someone who subscribes to a utilitarian perspective say about the policy? What about someone who subscribes to deontological ethics?

2. Is this policy a "slippery slope" to forbidding other types of activities? What if the policy tested for alcohol instead? What if the policy prohibited unhealthy eating habits and tested for high blood pressure and cholesterol? What if the policy was extended to forbid exposure to the sun or even tanning beds? What about forbidding risky sports?

3. What do you think of the policy of paying for any type of smoking cessation program? Should the department pay for things like hypnosis or acupuncture therapies that may not be scientifically validated? Is this a good use of state resources? What if the policy had stated that the department would only pay for medically prescribed smoking cessation therapies?

4. Should the legislature get involved in the situation, or is this strictly an internal policy matter? Does Dr. Billingsley have a right to know which of his employees contacted state legislators? Why or why not? Is it ethical for the legislators to withhold the names of the employees, or does Dr. Billingsley have a right to face his accusers, so to speak? Do public employees have a right to protest a department's policy or is that insubordination? Why or why not?

CASE 29: PRENATAL CARE FOR ILLEGAL IMMIGRANTS

Early in the legislative session, State Representative Randy Richards held a press conference to discuss his proposed bill that would prevent state agencies and other health care providers from offering prenatal care to illegal immigrants and billing the cost to Medicaid. According to Representative Richards, "Providing prenatal care to illegal immigrants and then billing that cost to Medicaid is committing fraud. We must not blur the lines between personhood and citizenship in this state. It is my belief that providing any such benefits to illegal immigrants is serious violation of federal law."

After his brief remarks, Representative Richards opened the floor for questions. Ed Stevens with the *Times Daily* asked, "Mr. Representative, isn't it true that the children of the mother are U.S. citizens if born here, regardless of the immigration status of the mother?"

"That is true Ed; however, the care is being provided to the mother herself, and there is no guarantee that the child will in fact be born here, so he or she may or may not ultimately become an American citizen. Besides, that's not the point. These people are here illegally, and to continue to provide services to them just encourages them to break the law. We must break this cycle of encouraging lawlessness!"

"But, Representative Richards, can't we assume that a significant number of these women will ultimately give birth to children here who *will be* U.S. citizens?" asked Gina Harper from Channel 5 News.

"Again, that is not the point. If they are ultimately born here then the children are, as Americans, entitled to benefits; however, many of us believe that the law needs to be changed so that a child has to be born to at least one American parent in order to get citizenship" With that reply, he ended the press conference.

After the Richards press conference, a number of reporters started contacting Mike Foley, the Executive Director of the state's Health Care Authority. The Health Care Authority is the state agency charged with administering the federal Medicaid program in the state. As a result of the number of calls, Mike reluctantly agreed to hold a brief press conference on the issue the day after the Richards press conference.

At 3:30 p.m. Mike met with reporters in the Authority's large conference room. Mike began by saying, "I don't have any opening remarks regarding Representative Richards's proposed legislation, but I will be happy to answer anyone's questions concerning the current program and how we administer it in the state today."

"Mr. Foley, in your opinion is it Medicaid fraud for the state to pay for prenatal care for illegal immigrants?" asked June Adkins from Channel 9 Action News.

"No, in fact the president and the Centers for Medicare and Medicaid Services have both issued interpretations of Title XIX of the Social Security Act that say that we should offer prenatal care under the program regardless of a woman's citizenship or immigration status," replied Mike.

Gina Harper from Channel 5 News then asked, "Well then, where is Representative Richards getting his information that it's committing fraud?"

"I can't answer that, Gina. You would have to ask Representative Richards about that. Perhaps he knows something I don't, but prior to this conference I went back and reviewed both the president's and CMS's interpretations of the statute."

"If you don't mind, Mr. Foley, what is your personal opinion on providing prenatal care to illegal immigrants?" asked Ed Stevens.

"Well, Ed, the cost of providing really good prenatal care for any woman who qualifies for Medicaid is less than $1,000. Studies show that good prenatal care decreases the risk that a child will be born with a serious medical condition. Any child born with a serious medical condition will cost well over $130,000 to treat. As you know, any child born here gets U.S. citizenship and would surely qualify for Medicaid if his or her parents cannot afford to pay, regardless of the parents' citizenship or immigration status. It would seem to me that it just makes good economic sense to provide these people with the proper care. As the old adage goes, 'an ounce of prevention is worth a pound of cure,'" replied Mike.

"Do you agree with Representative Richards that by providing services for illegal immigrants we are encouraging them to come here and break the law?" Stevens asked.

"You know, Ed, that is really beyond the scope of this conference. It really doesn't matter how I feel about Representative Richards's personal beliefs regarding immigration. It's simply my job to administer the program according to federal and state statutes and regulations. At this time, the state has simply mandated that the agency administer the program according to federal regulations and guidelines."

After Mike's press conference, Representative Richards went ballistic. He issued a statement on his official letterhead that read in part, "Mr. Foley was completely out of line. He had no business commenting on legislation that I am sponsoring. It's Mr. Foley's job to administer the program and if the legislature wants to implement restrictions on who qualifies for the program, then that is the purview of the legislature. I have sent a demand to Mr. Foley's boss, the state's Secretary of Health and Human Services, demanding that Mr. Foley retract his statements and issue an apology or be forced to resign as executive director of the Health Care Authority."

Mike, who was covered under the state's merit-protection plan, refused to retract his statements or issue an apology. According to Mike, "I did nothing wrong. The press asked for information on the plan, and I provided it. I did not state my personal beliefs and try to pass them off as the state's official stance on this issue. I simply commented about the current state of the program and cited statistics regarding prenatal care and the cost of caring for a child who is an American citizen should he or she suffer due to a lack of good prenatal care."

In response to Mike's lack of an apology, Representative Richards introduced a bill to remove the executive director's merit-protected status and make the position a governor's appointment with senate confirmation.

DISCUSSION QUESTIONS

1. In holding his own press conference, did Mike act unethically? To what extent should public employees refrain from publicly contradicting elected officials? Should the First Amendment protect such employees who speak out against elected officials, or should the official (in his or her official capacity) refrain from making such remarks? Would it matter if the official made the remarks to a reporter while off the clock and not at his official state office?
2. Can you cite an ethical theory that would support Representative Richards's position? How does this theory support his position? What ethical theory can be used to oppose the representative's position and why?
3. To what extent should elected officials be allowed to revise a state's merit-protection policy to exempt specific personnel from its coverage? If the legislature agreed that the position was one that should be exempt from coverage, should such exemption apply to the office's current incumbent, or should the current employee be covered by the original terms of his or her employment?
4. Both Representative Richards and Mike Foley are state officials wrestling with what is essentially a federal responsibility. In terms of immigration policy, what could elected leaders and public administrators at the federal level do to relieve the burdens of their counterparts at state and local levels? Speculate on why this is not happening.

CASE 30: PRIVATIZING THE COUNTY HOSPITAL

The board of physicians of the Green River County Hospital convened for their monthly meeting to discuss cases and hospital business. The big issue at hand was the proposal to turn over management of the hospital to a private contractor, namely Four Corners Health Partners (FCHP). It was a small outfit that had started buying up health facilities in the Colorado Plateau region, but was quickly expanding into other areas of the country. For public health care institutions, FCHP was now offering consulting services and, in this case, actual management of the county hospital.

The county commission had asked the board of physicians for its recommendations. The Director of Medical Staff, Dr. Melvin Wood called the meeting to order.

"The first item on our agenda is preparing a response to the county commission's inquiry. They want our perspective on the contract as proposed by FCHP for management of this hospital. Who would like to speak first?"

Several doctors raised their hands, but the director recognized Dr. Sophia Kopper, the senior physician on staff.

"Most of us here have already heard from colleagues and friends who work in facilities owned or managed by FCHP. The picture isn't pretty. FCHP does appear to deliver on its mission of lowering costs but it does so at the expense of patient care. The people I've talked to are frankly too scared to come out in the open and voice their concerns for fear of losing their jobs. My own independent research has revealed that FCHP has been involved in numerous scandals. Their public relations and lobbying efforts appear to be extremely effective in squelching complaints before they come to the public's attention. I think this outfit is unethical. We should tell the county commissioners that we unequivocally oppose this deal."

"Sophia, they're talking about closing this hospital. We may not have any alternative," said Dr. Wood.

"Mel, do you know if the county commission has explored other companies?" asked Dr. Kopper.

"No, I don't. Let's face it though, we are in a sparsely populated part of the country and I doubt that many companies would want to operate here."

Dr. Kopper did not respond. Her eyes glanced around at the other physicians.

Finally, Dr. Wood asked if anyone was in favor of recommending approval of the contract. Only Dr. Kopper responded.

"Mel, we have all met informally before coming here. All of us are in agreement that, as our representative, you should write a strong memo saying that we are unanimous in our objection to signing a contract with FCHP. I so move."

Several physicians simultaneously seconded the motion.

"We have a motion on the floor. All those in favor say Aye." Dr. Wood was met with a resounding chorus of voices.

"All those opposed say Nay." The room was silent.

"All right, I'll prepare a memo and forward it to the commission."

Later that day, Dr. Wood had lunch with the hospital administrator and a representative from FCHP.

When the administrator left to visit the restroom, the FCHP representative said to Dr. Wood, "I'm aware that your staff physicians have some reservations about our company. I can assure youz, Dr. Wood, that any problems we may have had in other jurisdictions have just been growing pains. We're a good company. Your administrator is eligible for retirement and I doubt that he will make the move to FCHP, should we get the contract. For somebody like you, however, I believe you will find an opportunity to come and grow with our company. You already have management experience and we like what we see. I'm sure that we could come to some arrangement about a significant increase in salary, not to mention stock options. Keep that in mind while you write the report."

Dr. Wood was thankful that at just that moment, the hospital administrator came back to the table.

Later that day, Dr. Wood looked over the accounting books and agreed with the county budget office that the hospital could not continue under the current financial arrangements. As he wrote the letter to the county commissioners, he deliberately softened the objections of the Green River County Hospital Board of Physicians.

DISCUSSION QUESTIONS

1. Comment on the suggestion that FCHP is the only viable alternative. What does this imply about the actual need for a hospital in this sparsely populated county? What does this imply about the priorities of the county commissioners? What other options might be considered?
2. Evaluate the position taken by Dr. Kopper and the other physicians. Does their responsibility as advisors extend beyond evaluation of patient care? What other issues should they consider?
3. List three possible motivations behind Dr. Wood's softening of the objections of the medical staff. Are any of them defensible from either an ethical or a managerial standpoint?
4. How would you react to the *quid pro quo* suggestion from the FCHP representative while the administrator was out of the room? Under what conditions, if any, would it be ethical for FCHP to employ such tactics in pursuing the contract?

Planning and Economic Development

CASE 31: TOURISM ADVERTISEMENT

Last February, tourism officials initiated a new advertising campaign to increase public awareness of the state's growing tourism industry. In a press release distributed to state and regional newspapers, the state Tourism Director, Janet Jeffreys announced, "Our spring tourism campaign is an effort to promote the state as the destination of choice for not only our own citizens, but also for those travelers from neighboring states."

Later, during a press conference of gubernatorial cabinet secretaries, a skeptical reporter from *The Daily Progressive*, the state's most politically liberal newspaper asked, "Isn't this a form of corporate welfare? Should we really be spending tax dollars to promote tourism when we have so many more pressing problems such as minimizing pollution, taking care of our urban poor, and getting adequate health care out to our rural communities?"

Jeffreys responded, "We know that for every dollar we invest in promoting tourism, more than $20 comes back to the state."

The next day, the following boldfaced headline appeared in *The Daily Progressive*: Tourism Ad Campaign is Butt of Criticism!

The story revealed that a small group of concerned citizens was protesting the new tourism and recreation guide. This slick publication featured glossy photographs and several articles about various attractions in the state. A new guide is distributed each year at the traveler information sites near the state line on incoming major highways and is sent by mail to those who call a toll free number or sign up on the state's Web site. The group's objection centered around an advertisement on the inside back cover. It showed a full-page photograph of a plumber, bending over to work on some pipes below a kitchen sink. A somewhat agitated housewife looks on awkwardly at the plumber's backside. Large letters at the top of the photograph asks, "If your free time is not all it's cracked up to be, take a break in our state."

"This is an incredibly tasteless advertisement!" screamed Charles Johnson, "What kind of image does this send about our state?" As leader of the protest group, he began calling for the immediate ouster of Janet Jeffreys as tourism director.

"I had no idea." Janet told reporters when she turned to the back page of the publication. After her obvious initial shock, she promised to look into the matter. But when she spoke to her advisors, they informed her that 225,000 copies of the guide had already been delivered to her office, ready for statewide distribution. She called a meeting of her senior staff. During the meeting, Bill Palmer, the public relations officer, took responsibility for the ad. He said, "We hired the best public relations firm available and they came up with this idea. I thought it was funny. Frankly, I still do. Doesn't anybody have a sense of humor anymore?"

"Well, I don't think it's funny that we've given *The Daily Progressive* something that they can sensationalize," Janet retorted. "We've got to do something and quick. What are our options? I need to make a decision sometime tomorrow, preferably early. Give me the information as you get it."

That afternoon, her staff forwarded to her initial reports which were not encouraging. The Legal Division researched the problem and concluded that since the Tourism Department had been provided the opportunity to proofread the final draft, it was contractually obligated to pay the $55,000 bill. The Purchasing Division estimated that it would cost about $25,000 to reprint and reattach the back cover. Operations staff concluded that reprinting the entire recreation guide was not feasible since it had to be distributed before the spring camping season and in time for travelers to begin planning their summer vacations. Janet felt all good options had been closed off.

To make matters worse, one of the local television stations featured the Tourism fiasco during its evening news hour as part of an ongoing series on government waste. This particular report not only slammed Janet for the current situation, but reminded viewers about an ill-fated purchase the previous year by the Tourism Department. In that instance, the Tourism Department had partnered with one of the local communities to sponsor a "Harvest Homecoming Balloon Festival," which had been scheduled for late autumn. Unfortunately, it was canceled three weeks prior to the appointed time because the contractor that made arrangements for the balloons had gone bankrupt. At the time, Janet was pleased that they were able to call the program off in sufficient time to prevent the mass mailing of invitations to area residents. She was even able to cancel that printing order, but was forced to accept the procurement of several thousand gold embossed stickers of the state seal that were intended for placement on the outside envelopes holding the planned engraved invitations. The same television station at the time had publicly ridiculed the agency for going to such extravagance in the first place, and prominently featured the ultimate waste of the high-priced state seals.

Before she turned in for bed that night, the governor's appointment secretary called her and asked if she would be available for a meeting with the governor the next day. Unless she and her staff could think of something quickly, Janet assumed that the governor would be asking for her resignation.

DISCUSSION QUESTIONS

1. Funny and/or sexy ads are frequently used by the private sector to promote business. Such ad campaigns are often successful. Are such ad campaigns appropriate for a state entity? What ethical theories can be cited for and against the use of such an advertising campaign?
2. Given the limited resources of most state government and the overwhelming need for basic services for infrastructure and the poor, is promoting tourism ethical? Should such promotion be left to the private sector that benefits from it? Why or why not?
3. Mistakes of judgment are inevitable. Is it fair or moral to fire a political employee over a mistake in order to appease the media or the public? What if the employee is a merit-protected employee? Given our high tech world, where information is transmitted instantly to thousands of people, do the media play too big a role in public policy and decisions? Is it ethically defensible for a newspaper or other news media to try to embarrass a public agency in one area because its editorial policy is at odds with the agency in other areas?
4. Imagine that you worked for Janet. What advice would you give her? What creative solutions can you generate that would serve as viable responses to this situation?

CASE 32: A REASONABLE OFFER

Jacob's oldest and dearest friend Alan called on the phone. "Hey, Jacob, I have a question that I think you could help answer."

"Let me hear it."

"Well, I know you're on the board overseeing the new crosstown corridor project. As you know, the new plan means that they're going to be cutting across the south edge of my property."

"Yes."

"I just got this letter and it says that the development board has appraised that part of my property at $67,850." Alan paused and then continued, "It says here that I can contest this appraisal value if I attend the upcoming meeting of the board. But if I decided to exercise that right that it could delay my receiving compensation and I would risk getting an even lower offer if a future appraisal went down. What I want to know is whether I should accept this initial offer or press for more money at that upcoming hearing."

Jacob was privy to the board's decision that anyone unwilling to accept the initial offer would automatically receive a new offer of 20 percent above the appraisal. Of course the board held that decision to be confidential information while negotiations were still in progress. He knew that he wouldn't tell Alan the specifics of the development board's strategy. His dilemma was whether he should lead his friend to accept the initial offer, give him some subtle signal to hold out for a higher sum, or just say nothing.

DISCUSSION QUESTIONS

1. What are the competing values and role conflicts inherent in this case?
2. What could be the logic behind the board's decision to automatically increase the offer to anyone unwilling to accept the initial offer? Does this approach violate any ethical principles? Be specific and explain your response fully.
3. Is it ethical for Alan to ask Jacob for advice on this matter? Describe three different scenarios in which this issue could drive a wedge between the long-time friends.
4. What issues must Jacob consider before answering? How would a consequentialist approach this problem? From the development board's perspective, what are the legal and financial ramifications of a signal from Jacob to hold out for a higher sum?

CASE 33: SHOOTOUT AT THE ZONING COMMISSION: MEGASTORE V. THE PHARMACISTS

"Let's call this meeting to order." The chair of the Mt. Chinle Area Zoning Commission readjusted his microphone before speaking again. "First item on the agenda is the request for development of Parcel Six. The land description and zoning proposal are in your packets. We are continuing with those in support of the development and will finish with those against—hopefully all can have their say this morning. First up is City Manager Gracie Miller. You now have the floor."

"Thanks, Commissioner Boyd. My staff and I have reviewed this proposal for the past several months. While not taking away from any of the reservations that other citizens might have about this SuperCenter locating in our town, on balance, we think that this will be a net benefit for our community. The MegaStore Corporation has acquiesced to most of our architectural and landscaping requirements. The new building will complement the unique style of buildings that grace our community. The building is designed to be severable into smaller units should MegaStore decide to vacate at some future point."

"We also believe that there will be a significant increase in our sales tax by allowing this store to locate within our city limits. We do foresee that it will have some negative impact on a few of our downtown businesses, but most should be able to share in the predicted prosperity. We think that it will draw a lot of tourists and campers and, most of all, those coming to our area to fish at Lake Chinle. In other words, we'll be getting a lot of new commercial traffic that in the past has tended to bypass our small town. This proposed store should bring a measurable increase in employment opportunities—both minimum wage and entry-level professional positions. For these reasons and others listed in our report, we recommend approval of this zoning request."

"Thank you, Ms. Miller," said Commissioner Boyd. "Anyone else like to speak on behalf of this proposal? No? Any of you representatives of MegaStore want to speak again before I turn it over to the other side? No? Okay. The chair now recognizes David Burchfield."

"Thanks Commissioner. My name is David Burchfield and I represent Chinle Citizens for Controlled Growth. As our name suggests, we are a group of citizens who have concerns about the mindless pro-growth mindset that has dominated our town leaders for the past several years. Chinle is a traditional community and we have been able to retain much of our old world charm by resisting encroachment from big land developers in the past. This respect for our past maintains our quality of life. It makes our town unique. And that has economic implications. If we're just like every other town with a MegaStore SuperCenter or a McDonalds, what makes us different? Why would anyone want to visit here? We're a tourist destination of choice because we offer a break from everywhere else. In this day and age, that's saying something. My assistant is handing you some of our literature which will further outline our concerns about this proposal. Thank you for your time."

"Okay, the chair now recognizes Marty Caston, who represents the Chinle Chamber of Commerce," said Commissioner Boyd.

"Hello. I'm Marty Caston. It's my privilege today to speak on behalf of the several small businesses that operate here in Chinle. Many of us are fierce competitors for the dollars in this town, but today we speak with one voice in opposition to the proposed MegaStore location. It would completely devastate our downtown. The very spirit and life of our community would be drained. The vitality that we know and love and experience every day in or downtown area would disappear in a matter of months after the opening of a MegaStore SuperCenter. Most importantly, you should consider that we currently have a very healthy and competitive business environment. We have several restaurants. We have two neighborhood grocery stores. We have a pharmacy on the east side of the city and another on the west side. We have two hardware stores both with knowledgeable sales staff. Unlike shopping in a MegaStore, you don't have to talk to some kid who's just going to read the package to you. You get real advice. Sure, MegaStore may offer some cheaper products, but what's the real cost? We have three different garages to help maintain your vehicle, with service people who really care about your business. Once MegaStore prices every one of our longstanding businesses into bankruptcy, they'll just raise their prices without consequence. Our citizens will have no choice. We strongly recommend that you reject this proposal. Some of you on this commission are elected leaders and we would like you to remember who finances your elections, promotes your campaigns, and turns out at the polls. We very much appreciate allowing this time to make our concerns known."

"That ends our slate of scheduled speakers this morning. Does anyone want to add anything else before we proceed into executive session?" asked Commissioner Boyd.

"Yes, if I may?"

Commissioner Boyd then recognized the MegaStore representative.

"Hello, once again, my name is Archie Golde and I'm an attorney with MegaStore. I have worked for the past four years easing the transition of MegaStore SuperCenters into new communities. Our experience is that existing businesses reshuffle and readjust as we enter the market. As with any new blood in a business community, there are some challenges and we do not apologize for being fierce competition. But it doesn't have to be a win-lose situation. Most businesses adapt quickly and prosper in spite of our presence and often because of it. I would like to rebut one point in particular about the so-called competition in this town. Mr. Caston mentioned the two pharmacies here in Chinle. Let me remind you before you go into executive session that you are here to serve the citizens. This is an aging community. There are a disproportionate number of senior citizens in Chinle. I find it odd that these two pharmacies—these so-called competitors—price their prescription medicines in almost exactly the same way. Here's a chart with the price for five of the most popular prescription medicines. The two left hand columns are the Mt. Chinle pharmacies and the right hand column is the average price at most MegaStore pharmacies in this state."

Golde then placed a tripod stand with a large white chart with the following information:

	Mt. Chinle Drug	Harper's Pharmacy	MegaStore
1. Lipitor (20 mg)	$299.00	$296.00	$131.00
2. Nexium (40 mg)	$240.00	$236.00	$175.00
3. Prevacid (30 mg)	$201.00	$195.38	$135.00
4. Singulair (10 mg)	$187.00	$194.00	$120.00
5. Plavix (75 mg)	$210.00	$216.00	$144.21

Golde then continued, "As you can plainly see, these two charming, old world apothecaries are gouging the citizens of this town. I'm not making an accusation here, but you should not just ask why their prices are so far beyond a reasonable profit margin, but also why do these two so-called competitors have remarkably similar pricing schemes? Could there perhaps be a cozy gentlemen's agreement going on here? So before you make your vote on what businesses would be best for the citizens of Chinle, keep in mind which business will really contribute to the well-being and quality of life for the people in this area. Thank you very much for your attention and your time."

DISCUSSION QUESTIONS

1. In your opinion, is David Burchfield's concern valid? What about Marty Caston's assertion of democratic principles? What processes and principles should Commissioner Boyd rely on if his reasoned judgment runs counter to his constituents' wishes?

2. Evaluate the role of Gracie Miller and her staff in this political process. Is there anything inherent in the city manager's position that would tend to bias her advice on matters concerning economic development and growth? How much weight should be given to Gracie's advice? In reality, how much weight is normally given to the city manager's advice? Why is this?

3. How persuasive are Archie's price comparisons? Is the use of data more persuasive than abstract economic theories? What theory does Archie offer to counter the anti-competition theory offered by Marty? Is Archie wise to suggest this line of reasoning? Is he in fact appealing to higher ethical levels? What should be the response of the opponents to this development?
4. Promoters of economic development often find themselves challenging the existing order. How do city leaders balance progress with tradition? How much weight should be given to longstanding loyal residents of a community versus potential benefits promised by enthusiastic newcomers?

CASE 34: COMPLIMENTARY SODA DRINKS FOR BUS DRIVERS

The new outdoor amphitheatre at the state park had turned out to be an incredible success. On most Friday and Saturday evenings during the summer, the amphitheatre was home to a stage play celebrating the early history of statehood. On other days, outdoor concerts often featuring well-known entertainers filled the 4,000-seat amphitheatre to capacity. Many times, the box office sold more tickets than seats and let families and couples settle down with blankets on the grassy outskirts of the amphitheatre. As theatre manager, Bill Jefferson was extremely proud of how the amphitheatre had become so important to the community and to the state. It was quickly becoming a top regional tourist attraction. The association of bus drivers had just given the amphitheatre its highest award.

The press release by the bus association included a Web link for more information about the award. That caught the attention of Representative Sparks who was over the Parks & Tourism Committee in the state legislature. There he found a blog in which one bus driver had described the state park and the amphitheatre as a pleasure to visit. He said specifically, "They know how to treat us bus drivers. They recognize that we're on the job and aren't there for our leisure, so they very nicely give us complimentary soda drinks and even let us have free barbecue sandwiches and hot dogs if we haven't already eaten dinner."

Sparks called Jefferson and let him know that "it's illegal for a state employee to provide free products or services to one citizen, if other citizens are charged for them."

Jefferson explained, "That may be so, but in the outdoor summer-stock business, it helps to keep the bus drivers happy if you want to bring in business. It's just standard operating procedure in this kind of setup, whether it's public or private. We try to treat the bus drivers like gold. You would be surprised how many traveling groups take the suggestions of bus drivers and tour guides."

"I hear you," Sparks said, "and I understand where you're coming from. On the other hand, you know some busybody is going to get wind of this and make it into some boondoggle scandal. I think you should cut it out or at least keep it on the QT."

DISCUSSION QUESTIONS

1. If a public entity decides to engage in the equivalent of a business venture, should it be able to compete in the same manner as its competitors? Or is there a special mandate for public organizations to meet a higher or a different standard? Should public organizations be completely restrained from competing with businesses?
2. Describe three ethically questionable activities taking place in the story. Would any of them be problematic if the amphitheatre were a private sector enterprise? What advice would you give Bill Jefferson regarding the differences between private and public sector management?
3. Is Representative Sparks justified in characterizing someone who would object to the free sodas and sandwiches as a "busybody"? Is his advice to Bill Jefferson defensible from a legal standpoint? What does the advice reveal about the representative's moral compass?
4. How important to the success of the amphitheatre is the practice of giving things away to bus drivers? How would you weigh the risks against the benefits? Describe the criteria that would be appropriate when comparing alternative courses of action.

CASE 35: THE ETHANOL LOAN SUBSIDY

Melinda Marjino is a woman who sticks to her principles. After eight years in the state senate, she imposed "terms limits" on her own legislative career. Instead of running for re-election and a third term, she decided to enter the statewide race for treasurer. At every speech and campaign stop, Melinda emphasized her many accomplishments on the Accountability and Oversight Committee.

"Our state continues to face ethical challenges stemming from a culture of greed in the public arena," she would say. "As chair of the Oversight Committee, I have rooted out waste, fraud, and abuse that have drained our state coffers and caused us great embarrassment in the national media. Conflicts of interest have been lining the pockets of public officials, while chipping away at our faith in government."

Melinda's message and track record proved to be a winning combination, and she was soon sworn in as the state's forty-seventh treasurer. True to her principles, Melinda drew up a set of ethics guidelines that would apply to programs under her jurisdiction. Melinda's goal was to keep public officials from profiting as a result of taxpayer-funded programs. The first test of the stringent new policies turned out to be the state's Business Incentive Program (BIP). As Treasurer, Melinda is charged with implementing and overseeing the program.

Under the BIP program, state funds are deposited in selected banks at interest rates 3 percentage points lower than the typical deposit rate. For its part, the bank then passes along the 3 percentage point difference to businesses that seek out and qualify for the loans. The first entity to apply for the low-interest funding under BIP was the recently formed Corn Belt Ethanol Cooperative.

Corn Belt has an interesting history. The brainchild of Governor Eugene "Birdy" Birdwell, the cooperative is owned by over 700 shareholders, most of them farmers. In the beginning, however, getting the idea off the ground proved to be quite a struggle. An ambitious media campaign had failed to spark much interest or attract many investors. Then, with failure looming on the horizon, State Senator Mitch Dierdorff decided to put his money where his mouth was.

A long-time supporter of ethanol, Dierdorff stepped forward as Corn Belt's first high profile investor. He announced that his wife, Candy, would purchase one hundred shares. This was a symbolic gesture, intended to demonstrate confidence in the future of ethanol and signal the likelihood of ongoing legislative support as well. Other supporters appeared, including Governor Birdwell, who asked his brother Gary to buy shares in Corn Belt. Even Congressman Derby bought shares. Farmers took notice, and many decided to join in. Within a month Corn Belt had a full slate of officers in place. They prepared their application for an $82 million loan under the auspices of the state BIP, and mailed copies to the First Union Bank of DeSoto and the State Treasurer's office.

Corn Belt's application was approved by First Union within two weeks. News spread fast, and the price of Corn Belt shares began to move upward. Then came the bad news. The *DeSoto Herald* quoted Treasurer Marjino's extensive remarks from a news conference held earlier that day.

"My department's strict conflict of interest policy applies to all statewide projects," Marjino insisted. "Under the rules, no incentives can be given if the company has even a single investor who is a lawmaker, statewide elected official, state department director, or a parent, sibling, spouse, or child of any of those officials. This is the taxpayers' money, and I don't think it's right for legislators or elected officials to be able to access that benefit, which helps them profit directly."

DISCUSSION QUESTIONS

1. Corn Belt has yet to secure the funding to build its plant. If the politicians and their relatives don't sell their shares, or if Marjino doesn't ease up a bit, the future of Corn Belt becomes very uncertain. How should the officials respond to Treasurer Marjino's comments?

2. Marjino's critics point out that her rules are very strict compared to the Department of Agriculture's conflict of interest policy. Those rules, which apply to a tax credit program, specify that no conflict of interest exists as long as no official holds more than 10 percent of the total shares. Corn Belt passes this test. How should Marjino respond to these critics?

3. Gary Birdwell, the Governor's brother, believes the Treasurer's office should relax its policy, perhaps allowing up to 5 percent of investors to have political connections. What do you think of this type of compromise?

4. Can the motivations for a private investment be seen from a more altruistic perspective? That is, can someone risk their own money hoping for a profitable return, but still be motivated primarily to support a favorite cause such as

in this case with an emerging industry based on alternative fuels? Is this actually a conflict of interest that would cause the public to lose faith in their public leaders?

CASE 36: FREE BUILDING FOR TITAN TROUT SHOP

In order to stimulate investment in the old warehouse district downtown, the city council agreed to build a large, multi-level building. Specifically, city leaders were excited about attracting the popular Titan Trout Pro Shop to open up one of its famous outdoor and sports retail outlets. If Titan Trout executives agreed to the deal, they would lease the city-built building for at least ten years at below market prices. They would also allow Titan Trout to operate for the first five years tax free because of their willingness to locate in a blighted area of the city. It would be the first new opening of a major retail outlet in the downtown area in over thirty years. The mayor, who sat on the city council, and the city manager had been prime movers in arranging the deal. Titan Trout executives believed that the store's location next to two major interstate highways and the freeway loop around the metropolitan area would bring abundant traffic near the store. The city council seemed favorable to helping close the contract. Almost everyone seemed to be excited and enthusiastic about the potential of a Titan Trout Pro Shop to reinvigorate development in the run-down warehouse district area—*almost* everyone.

A group of owners who owned smaller shops catering to outdoor enthusiasts lined up before the city council on Tuesday morning during the time for new business. They complained that, although they had invested their monies and much of their lives in promoting their own businesses in the city, they did not get cozy lease arrangements or tax breaks. They believed that the Titan Trout Pro Shop would eventually steal too much of their business and they would not survive financially.

The Chamber of Commerce weighed in with its recommendation to approve the deal for Titan Trout over the objection of many of its own members. The belief was that it would be good for overall business in the city. Best of all, it would bring in new money from travelers who normally passed the city by. The Chamber believed that the economic benefits would ripple throughout the entire city economy.

DISCUSSION QUESTIONS

1. Are the owners of the smaller shops justified in their opposition to the arrangement? What could they have done differently to make their concerns weigh more heavily in the council's and city manager's decision process?
2. Do new investors in a community deserve special treatment? What ethical justification exists for the more favorable tax and lease treatment given to Titan? Are

council members obligated to follow any particular ethical principles in a situation like this?

3. Evaluate the process by which the decision was made. Is it ethically sound? Is there anything politically or financially suspect about the decision? What are the advantages and disadvantages of setting a precedent of this kind?

4. Under what ethical theory would the Chamber of Commerce agree to a proposal that would likely increase overall profits, but at the expense of a vocal minority of its own members?

Education Administration and Policy

CASE 37: CHANGING THE GRADE

Professor Karlsen looked at his spreadsheet one more time. He was running up against the deadline to turn in grades and needed to decide quickly about some students whose grades were on the margin. Of particular concern were two students, Robin Crittenden and Bill Madison. Robin had scored a 79.4 percent and Bill a 79.5 percent. Professor Karlsen finally decided against rounding up their grades to a B because his syllabus indicated that attendance would be taken into consideration only in view of marginal grades. Both Robin and Bill had missed over 50 percent of the class time. He liked both students, but he had to draw the line somewhere.

Shortly after he posted the grades to the university's central database, he received an urgent call from Robin, who had checked her grades online. She explained that she was a Native American and received a very generous scholarship from her tribe. "You need to know, Dr. Karlsen, that the money I get from this scholarship is what allows me to go to school."

"Well, you understand about my attendance policy?" he asked.

"Of course, and I don't have a good excuse except that it was my first semester in college and I just volunteered for way too many extracurricular activities. I just made it so difficult for myself to get to your early morning class on time," she said. "I was coming a lot more consistently toward the end of the semester and studying a lot more for the final exams. I was hoping you could give me the benefit of the doubt."

"I'll think about it and let you know later today."

DISCUSSION QUESTIONS

1. Who is really the "consumer" of higher education? Is it the student? If the institution is public, are the ultimate "consumers" the citizens of the state who provide

most of the funding? What if the institution is private? Can an argument be made that the "ultimate consumer" is the person who hires the college graduate thinking that he or she has attained a certain level of knowledge?

2. Based on your answers to the question above, is it ethical to change the grade? What about fairness to other students? Is it fair to raise Robin's grades when others may have come to class regularly and studied harder?

3. Should Professor Karlsen consider Robin's unique situation? Should Robin have thought about her scholarship before signing-up for some many extracurricular activities? What ethical theory can be cited in support of changing Robin's grade based on her need for the scholarship? What ethical theory can be cited in opposition to changing the grade?

4. During the Vietnam War, there was widespread speculation that "grade inflation" occurred on many college campuses in order to help males avoid the draft. If such grade inflation occurred, was that ethical?

CASE 38: THE SUPERINTENDENT'S SCANDAL

Porter Plantar, the recently hired Superintendent of the Mission City School District, enjoyed widespread support among parents and school board officials alike. Known for a "can-do" approach and more than a little impatience with bureaucracy, he had also made enemies along the way. Although Porter had been on the job only seven months, news stories that had begun to appear in the Mission City *Chronicle* were casting an unfavorable light on his administration. Most troublesome was the allegation that the superintendent was ignoring established procedures regarding the purchase of textbooks for the district. In fact, Assistant Superintendent Shelley Turkelson was quoted as saying that Porter engineered a "sweetheart deal" with one of the publishers. As a result, School Board member Dan Hebron, Porter's chief ally, proposed they meet over lunch to talk about the news stories. Porter was eager to give his side of the story, and suggested they get together at the high school. That Friday, Porter sat down with Dan at the only empty table in the cafeteria.

"Why is Shelley doing this?" Dan asked.

"I can't say for sure, Dan, but I do know that our working relationship has been lukewarm at best—sometimes downright chilly. And on a personal level, she seems very suspicious of everything I do."

"Do you think it has something to do with that reorganization of yours?" Dan prodded. "We all took heat from the PTA on that, not to mention the union."

"Oh, probably, I guess," Porter replied. "A lot of turf that used to be Shelley's got shifted to other people. I cut her out of the purchasing loop completely and took it over myself."

"Yes," said Dan, "I remember that decision. But she didn't seem very upset about it then. Has she been holding her tongue all this time?"

"I would say so, Dan. You know she was never in favor of hiring me. And then the reorganization caught her off guard. Ever since then, she has been very hostile—even in front of other people. I don't normally care about things like insubordination, because I have a thick skin. I must say, though, Shelley's confrontational behavior is beginning to annoy me. She's acting like she wants to provoke a fight."

"Well, we both know she's feeling pretty confident these days," said Dan. "The folks over at the *Chronicle* paint her as a whistleblower over the textbook deal. Have you thought about how you'll answer the allegations?" Porter put down his fork and squared his shoulders, bristling at the question.

"I don't have to give very much thought to it, Dan," Porter insisted. "I'll tell the truth, of course. The new contract with McCauley Publishing puts last year's deal with Drymon House to shame. We get new books instead of those moldy out-of-date ones. They provide tech resources and better supplements. Teachers are happier, students like them, and we actually saved money. So what if I didn't follow procedure?"

"Look, Porter," said Dan. "You know I approve of how you handle things. You get results, and that's what we want. But it might not look so bad if you had taken bids from other publishers too. Nothing against McCauley, but they are the only source you considered. And frankly it's embarrassing to keep hearing over and over again about your past relationship with the McCauley sales representative. Folks are saying it doesn't pass the smell test."

At the next School Board meeting Porter defended his actions. "I know it looks bad, but that can be said of so many things we do these days. Okay, so maybe it is a sweetheart deal. If I get what we need because I know someone, is that always bad? Should I spend more of the district's money than is necessary just to avoid the appearance of a conflict of interest? If I had opened this up to bids I would have bound us to all those crazy policies and we'd have been stuck with lousy books."

Shelley responded, "This is a classic case of using the ends to justify the means. Is that any way to safeguard the public trust? What kind of precedent are we setting here? The people need to be able to count on us to establish fair and rational procedures for spending their money. And we need to be held accountable for following them."

DISCUSSION QUESTIONS

1. Critique Porter's stance about the book contract. What ethical theories underlie Porter's perspective on getting the job done?
2. Critique Shelley Turkelson's response to Porter. Discuss Shelley's motivations, and whether or not they are relevant.
3. What should the school board do? Should they ask the district attorney to open a criminal investigation on the matter? Discuss the various courses of action available to the board and evaluate their potential effects on future book contracts, future lunch table discussions, and future candidate searches to fill leadership positions in the district.

4. Would Porter's leadership style be as much of a problem if he was an administrator over a private school? Why or why not?

CASE 39: GIFT CERTIFICATE FOR RECOMMENDATION LETTER

Professor Theo was sitting quietly in his office grading papers when his colleague, Professor Jaymes, poked her head in his door. "Do you have a minute?" she asked.

"Sure, come in and sit down."

"Did you write Susan Paulson a recommendation letter for that executive fellowship?"

"Yes," replied Dr. Theo. "I sent it in last week. In fact, she's obviously written me a thank you note." He pointed at the top envelope in his pile of daily mail.

"That's exactly what I wanted to talk to you about. I wrote her a letter, too, and she's also sent me a thank you note." Dr. Jaymes paused for dramatic effect. "Have you opened yours yet?"

"No." He then reached across his desk, got his thank you card, and opened it. "Oh my . . . she's given me what looks like a gift card."

"It is. It's from Starbucks and if it's like mine, the value is $30. You can check it online."

"Are you here because you're feeling uncomfortable about this?"

"A little. I mean, it feels like a bribe. You teach ethics and since you're now in the same boat, I was curious as to your take."

"Well, I have to think about it, but at first blush, I didn't know she was going to give me anything for my letter—much less something of monetary value. There's not even an implicit quid pro quo here. When I worked in state government, the rule was that you couldn't take anything from a vendor or lobbyist that you couldn't eat in one sitting. So yeah, I do feel a bit awkward about it, but I don't think it's such a big deal."

"Good, that's what I finally decided as well." Dr. Jaymes looked visibly relieved. "So, do you want to go out for coffee?"

DISCUSSION QUESTIONS

1. Why do professors agree to write letters of recommendation for students? How genuine or trustworthy are recommendation letters? How important are they in the selection process?
2. Under what conditions would you agree to write a letter for someone? How honest would you be? Would you be comfortable writing an unfavorable letter of reference?
3. Are these professors risking any adverse legal or personnel action by using the gift cards? What would their supervisors say about this? Would this set a precedent or create an expectation that letter writers should be thanked in a material way?
4. Is this an appropriate way to thank someone for writing a letter on your behalf? What are the implications if a "quid pro quo" is expected in a situation like this?

CASE 40: STATE UNIVERSITY FOOTBALL COACH AND THE WAYWARD TEAM

"As the highest paid public official in this state—he makes twice as much as the governor and even more than the physician who heads the state hospitals— he has a duty to keep his players in line. As football coach of our oldest and grandest institution of higher education, Coach Bratton should have taken a much greater interest in the extracurricular activities of the athlete-students under his charge. But no! When his players are involved in scandal after scandal, he places his head squarely in the sand where he can see no evil, do no evil." Grace Rybak, the athletic director put down the newspaper from which she was reading the lead editorial. "Do you want me to read from some of the papers in the other metropolitan areas?"

"No, that's quite enough," said Arnold Wikstrom, President of the university. "I'm a retired politician. I know all too well the games that the media likes to play in this town and in this state. Well, do you have any suggestions? Have you talked with Bratton about this latest scandal?"

"Yes, and he's pretty opinionated and also very angry about how this latest incident has been framed in the media," said Grace. "Bratton told me this morning that he wanted me to communicate two points to you. First, he says he is not the mother of these players. All of them are over eighteen. They're not babes in the woods. They're supposed to be adults. Second, he says that anyone can make accusations about anything, and he thinks with the series of problems that have come to light involving members of his team over the past several months—the drunk driving, the gambling incident, the fight in the parking lot—that these two young ladies and their willing accomplices in the media smell blood in the water. He says he's doubtful that the two players supposedly involved are even capable of rape. He wants you to hold back judgment until all the facts are in."

"Well, of course, but I'm getting a lot of pressure here."

Grace sighed, then continued, "This season has not been spectacular, but he's already won the national championship and almost invariably gets our team some prestigious bowl match-ups. He's a winning coach, and he's especially liked by those alumni who give big money. I wouldn't be too hasty in throwing him under the bus. There will be blowback from that as well."

"Damned if I do, damned if I don't. Well, what exactly are my options at this . . ." Arnold stopped talking when his Administrative Assistant walked in the door.

"I thought you might need to see this right away." She handed the president a paper.

"What's this?"

"It's a petition from the regular faculty calling for the termination of Coach Bratton. Oh, and Grace, too . . . as soon as possible."

DISCUSSION QUESTIONS

1. To what extent, if any, is a coach responsible for the actions of players? To what extent should Grace be held responsible for the actions or inactions of Coach

Bratton? Does it matter that the coach is paid a very high salary? Does the severity of an accusation against a player matter? Does the history of previous scandals matter? Explain your answer.

2. Evaluate the organizational structure of the typical large state university in terms of "principles" of administration like unity of command, span of control, etc. How much control can reasonably be expected? Can anything be done structurally to enhance the level of control over players' off-the-field behavior?

3. How much responsiveness to "pressure" should President Wikstrom show? How should the media situation be handled? Do you consider the faculty petition an overreaction? Why would the faculty petition call for Grace's termination rather than just Coach Bratton's? Is this justified? Why not ask for the resignation of President Wikstrom as well?

4. One of the ethical standards often applied to public service positions is that administrators should avoid even the "appearance of impropriety." Is that standard justifiable, and if so, should it apply in this instance?

CASE 41: WORKING EXTRA TO PAY YOUR OWN SALARY

Chairperson Courtney Dyer addressed her colleagues in the Department of Rehabilitative Sciences at the state's major research university: "I want to welcome all of you returning faculty and especially welcome the new members of our department. We're going to be walking through some new items of interest that are on our agenda today. We'll take a break midmorning and then continue through and have a working lunch. Hopefully, we'll be through with today's business by three or four o'clock this afternoon."

"The first item of business," she said, "is of course grants, funding, and research. I need to start off this first faculty meeting with a reality check. Let me put this as bluntly as I am able: As a faculty member here at the Health Sciences Center of the flagship university of this state, you are expected to be fully engaged in research and the acquisition of grants to fund that research. That is your number one priority. In a matter of speaking, you have to generate the funds that pay your salary. I have spoken with the Provost who informs me that our Department lags behind every other department at the Health Sciences Center in this area. This will change this academic year. If you are not able—for whatever reason—to get a grant written and awarded to fund your position, you will need to participate in faculty clinical practice and raise your own salary. Let me be clear on. . . ."

Dr. Catherine New raised her hand and Dr. Dyer looked a bit exasperated with the interruption. "Yes, Cathy, what is it?"

"Please excuse me for interrupting, but I really can't agree with your premise." Cathy looked around at all of her colleagues before starting again.

"We have heard this every year and I am the first to recognize the importance of research, and much of that can't go on without an appropriate level of grantsmanship. Something that tends to get missed is that we are more than just researchers. I believe our primary mission, and I am certain that the taxpayers who subsidize this university would overwhelmingly agree, is to train and educate the next generation of professional caregivers in the fields of allied health. We have the only physical therapy, occupational therapy, speech pathology, and audiology programs in the state. In fact, our university has fought tooth and nail to prevent other universities more focused on teaching than research from encroaching on our territory. And yet, you here today—and I'm sure you are just parroting the directives our administrators have told you to pass along—have the audacity to suggest that the only valuable work we engage in is research."

Cathy took a quick breath and then continued, "Colleagues outside of our department have reported they've been hearing the same things from their chairs and deans as well. Let's face it. As faculty at the Health Sciences Center, we are training—and I don't think that *training* is a bad word—we are training the very same health care providers who are going to be our future physicians, nurses, dentists, and therapists who are going to take care of us and our families in the not-so-distant future. That's not crazy. Most of us sitting around this table are in our fifties, some are even over sixty, and none of us is younger than forty. I've paid my dues in the clinical setting. I have led and continue to lead a very active research agenda with or without funding. So my goal is to pass along everything I can to our students. We should all be focused like a laser beam on that mission. We can't just slough it off and say that's the mission of the regional universities. They don't have medical schools. They don't have nursing programs at the RN level. They don't have dental schools. They don't have speech, and occupational, and physical therapy programs. We do! On the main campus of this so-called research university we have a law school. Sure, they teach the theory of the law and they do legal research. But they understand that their primary mission is to train law students to be future practicing attorneys. We don't even pay lip service to teaching our students anymore. What's happened to us? I'll tell you what, Dr. Dyer, if I wanted to raise the funds to pay my salary by participating in clinical practice, I'd rather get hired by one of the hospitals or therapy groups. You know I'd make a lot more money and work fewer hours. My first year students often make more money than I do. I think of my work here as a public service. Why is the Health Sciences Center failing to recognize the hard work that we do and the value that we deliver to this state every semester? Dr. Dyer, why aren't you in the face of each administrator in our chain of command, representing your colleagues here in the fine and noble profession of teaching?"

After Dr. Cathy New stopped her rant, she sat down. She had been so caught up with her unplanned reaction to the chair's admonitions she hadn't even realized that she had stood up at some point. Dr. Dyer's face was expressionless. The rest of the faculty sat in stunned silence. Finally, Dr. Bornkamm, the anatomy professor, began clapping. A few seconds later almost everyone in the room joined the applause.

DISCUSSION QUESTIONS

1. What are the positive aspects of a system where faculty members fund their own salaries? Does this expectation reflect any unstated assumptions on the part of the administrators of the Health Sciences Center?
2. If you were in Courtney Dyer's position as chair of the department, how would you handle the situation? Is it a good idea to be so blunt about the expectations? What management philosophy would you draw upon in dealing with the roomful of applause for someone taking a stand against administrative direction?
3. Consider Dr. Cathy New's position as the outspoken critic of the system. Was this meeting a good time to speak up, or should she have expressed her concerns in a less public manner? What are the possible ramifications awaiting Dr. New?
4. Evaluate the arguments employed in Dr. New's rant. Is the fact that they have "paid their dues" relevant? Is unfunded research as valuable as funded research? Does teaching really suffer, under these conditions, to the point that it becomes inadequate in terms of bringing the next generation of specialists up to speed? Or does research help improve teaching?

CASE 42: PROFESSOR DATING STUDENT

Just as Professor Paul Rabb was finishing his lecture on the latest anthropological research emphasizing musical forms of various African tribes on the western continent, a young lady opened the door and pointed to her watch.

"We'll pick this up next Tuesday. Make sure that you read the next chapter in the Medlar text and have a great weekend." As the class began filtering out, he motioned for his visitor to come on in. "Hi Sherry, hold on. Here take this, please." He handed her two thick volumes. We need to drop this stuff off in my office before we go."

"Hey, Sherry," said another student as she was leaving.

"Oh, hi, Theresa. I didn't know you were taking one of Paul's classes."

"Paul? I call him Dr. Rabb."

"I guess that's a privilege I have since I'm not one of his students."

"So what are you two up to?"

"We're about to go have a lunch date—maybe a picnic if I can talk Paul into it."

"See you both next week."

After Theresa left, Dr. Rabb asked, "So how do you know her?"

"We're in Dr. Adler's *Cultures of the Anasazi* class together."

"You mean you're a student at this university? And you're taking classes in my department?"

"I thought you knew. Why else would I have been at that lecture where we met? What's the problem? It's not like I'm in any of your courses."

DISCUSSION QUESTIONS

1. Is there an actual conflict of interest here, or perhaps the appearance of conflict of interest? Describe the interests that are potentially in conflict. How would Paul defend himself against accusations along these lines?

2. Evaluate Sherry's behavior. Is there anything wrong with exposing other students to the situation? What are the dangers for Sherry? Does this situation create any difficulties for Theresa, now that she has been made aware of it?
3. Aside from the potential issues involving conflict of interest, why might Paul react with concern? Is his behavior unprofessional in any way? What would be a prudent policy for the university to adopt concerning situations like this?
4. Universities strongly discourage professors from having romantic relationships with students, even though both are adults, under the theory that an inverse power relationship might compromise true consent. In your opinion, is this truly a consensual relationship?

To Protect and to Serve

CASE 43: ROUGH DAY IN TORNADO ALLEY

The series of tornadoes that had swept through the extensive urban area on the city's west side had left numerous families suffering in its wake. The rising sun soon revealed the full extent of the devastation. As the disaster coordinator, Craig Moran began barking out commands to the relief units. "We need to concentrate on the Oak Tree and Eskridge neighborhoods and then expand our operations from there."

As the crews started moving out, Craig's assistant was moved to ask, "Why are you focusing on the rich neighborhoods first. The poorer neighborhoods should at least be given equal attention. In fact, I bet they're suffering even more."

"I hear you," Craig responded, "but you have to realize that the heart of prosperity in this community is those wealthier neighborhoods and the businesses that serve them. If we don't get them up and running as soon as possible, everyone will suffer. With our limited resources, we have to be choosy where we direct our efforts. We'll get to the other parts of the city in time."

Craig's assistant looked unsettled.

After some uncomfortable silence, Craig finally said, "Okay, tell you what. The churches and nonprofits should be arriving soon. Direct them to the other parts of the city. But the main equipment, materials, relief supplies, and manpower need to go to Oak Tree and then to Eskridge. When the Feds arrive, you send 'em that way too. Got that?"

DISCUSSION QUESTIONS

1. What should be the appropriate guiding principles for disaster coordination? What would be a reasonable set of criteria for prioritizing activities? To what extent should economics play a role?
2. What kinds of ethical issues pertain to Craig's decision? What are some likely effects of leaving the poor part of town unattended in the storm's immediate aftermath?

3. In your opinion, is Craig exercising due diligence in his duties? Explain your answer.

4. Is it a good idea for a disaster coordinator to have discretion regarding where to focus the response efforts? What are some other processes that could be employed to increase the likelihood of better decision making?

CASE 44: PORNOGRAPHY AND THE POLICE CHIEF'S WIFE

Stigler is a small rural town of 10,000 inhabitants in the buckle of the Bible belt. A welcome sign to the community sponsored by the Stigler Interfaith League says, "Welcome to Stigler, home of over 35 churches." The vast majority of the population of the community identify themselves as protestant born-again Christians.

In January, Stigler hired a new police chief named Jim Barnes who was not a native of Stigler, but had impressive credentials. For the first time in its history, the city hired an outsider for the position.

Jim and his wife, Janis, moved to the city shortly after he was offered the position, but they never really fit in with the local population. Many of the town's leaders asked Jim and Janis Barnes to attend church with them; however, they always declined these invitations.

Six months after the Barneses moved to Stigler, several members of the community discovered that Janis had been a nude model and had operated an Internet Web site on which she posted pictures of herself and other nude individuals.

News of Janis's Web site spread quickly throughout the small community. A large group of citizens decided that Jim had to go; they attended the next city council meeting. The group was so large that it filled not only the council's chambers but also the hallway outside and spilled out on to the street in front of city hall. Over seventy-five people asked to address the council.

One woman named Viola Jones told the council, "My twelve-year-old granddaughter came home yesterday, and said 'Grandma, they said at school today that the police chief's wife is a porno queen.' He is supposed to be someone who children look up to and respect. This has made a mockery of his high office, and he should be fired."

The editor of the local paper, Ed Tweety, told the council, "I have investigated this Web site and what we have here is beyond disgusting. Imagine hardcore pornography, and this stuff is ten times worse." In fact, Janis's Web site displayed only nude photographs, and was hardly "hardcore."

The council went into executive session and met with the city attorney. Twenty minutes later, they emerged from the session and Mayor Ray Jones read the following statement, "We the members of the City Council of Stigler do not support pornography. However, we respect the First Amendment rights of all citizens as adjudicated by the United States Supreme Court. No law has been broken, and Chief Barnes did not participate in this activity. Therefore, no action will be taken to remove Chief Barnes from office."

Most of the citizens present were outraged by the action of the council, and prominent members of the community began an effort to recall all members of the council the next day.

DISCUSSION QUESTIONS

1. Did the council act ethically in this situation? Why or why not? Justify your answer.
2. Should Chief Barnes have resigned? Is it ethical for him to stay in office? Why or why not?
3. To what extent should community leaders' values reflect the values of the community in which they serve? Even though no law has been broken, given the deeply held values of the community should Jim be allowed to continue in office? The First Amendment is also a deeply held value among most Americans. Are the citizens of Stigler ignoring this value? When two deeply held values conflict, how should one decide which one to follow?
4. To what extent should public officials be accountable for the behaviors of members of their families? Should public officials and their families be held to a higher standard?

CASE 45: NUKES TRAVEL CROSS COUNTRY

"This isn't the first time this has happened," Major Nalbandian thought to himself as he filed the confidential personnel report.

Under orders from the munitions squadron commander, the ground crew at Andrews Air Force Base had sent a package of six cruise missiles to Edwards Air Force Base where they were scheduled for immediate decommission. The problem was that the personnel at Andrews AFB failed to remove the nuclear warheads before transport as required by established safety protocols. The half-dozen cruise missiles with warheads attached were loaded into a B-52 bomber. Its flight path took it over 2500 miles across eleven different states. The cockpit crew remained unaware of their cargo until they landed in California almost 6 hours later.

Major Nalbandian just shook his head and thought to himself, "This head of munitions has just killed any future promotions, but they're letting him keep his command without much consequence besides this minor demerit in his personnel file. He's just proven that he shouldn't be allowed anywhere near nuclear weapons." Nalbandian glanced over at his morning copy of the *New York Times*. "I wonder if I should give someone there a call?" he thought.

DISCUSSION QUESTIONS

1. Assuming Nalbandian is correct about the munitions squadron commander, in that "he shouldn't be allowed anywhere near nuclear weapons," what might be the justifications for letting keep his command? What legal issues might arise if he were stripped of his command?

2. Considering that this is not the first time this has happened, what might be inferred about the squadron commander's superiors? Discuss the organizational, ethical, and managerial objectives at stake.
3. What would be the appropriate personnel action regarding the munitions commander? What are the possible alternatives? What would be the best process for deciding what to do?
4. Should Nalbandian call the press? Why or why not?

CASE 46: HIGHWAY PATROL OFFICER SELLS BENEFIT TICKETS

Arlene French had just put her baby daughter down for an afternoon nap when the doorbell rang. She was relieved that the baby didn't wake up and fuss. When she answered the door, Arlene was surprised to find a state trooper in full dress uniform standing on her front porch. "What's wrong officer?"

"Ma'am, I am Captain Derek Axelrod and I'm here to invite you and your husband or anyone else in your household that you care about to come to the Annual Trooper's Ball. It's going to be held next month on the first Saturday evening at 6:30 PM. It's just down the road here a coupla miles at the ol' Antler Lodge. Tickets are just $25 apiece and you would be helping to support not only the Troopers Association but we'll also be giving money to a local children's charity. Can I put your name down for two tickets?"

"Oh, well, this is not the best time . . ."

"If you're worried about paying now, don't worry. As long as we get your pledge we will reserve the tickets for you, and you can pay at the door. It's going to be real fun. We'll have a live band and good food. You and your husband can have a date night and dance the night away. Best of all, you'll be showing your support for those men and women who put their lives on the line for you and yours every day. And it's for the children."

"Honestly, I don't know if we have it in our budget. We'd have to get babysitting and . . . I really need to talk with my husband before committing. Thank you." Arlene started to close the door.

"I am sure that he would be pleased as punch that you showed the initiative here. Let me hand you this pen and paper. If you'll just sign right there, we'll have two tickets waitin' for ya. I'll try to remind you personally the day before."

DISCUSSION QUESTIONS

1. Evaluate Captain Axelrod's decision to sell tickets to the ball while in full uniform. How do you feel about his decision to go door to door? Are his persuasive tactics justifiable from an ethical perspective? Why or why not?
2. What would normally be the goals and objectives of a Troopers Association? Are these goals and objectives transparent? Are they controversial in any way? In what ways might a Troopers Association find itself in a conflict of interest?

3. What are Arlene's most immediate concerns? How do you suppose her husband will react when she tells him the story? What options would be available to citizens who feel uncomfortable with, or angry about, Captain Axelrod's approach?
4. Would it be ethical for Arlene to sign the pledge so that the trooper will leave, and then not show up that evening to purchase the tickets? Why or why not? What would you do in a similar circumstance?

CASE 47: CYBER TERRORISM

"Good morning everyone. Please excuse us for interrupting your work, but this will just take a second. I'd like to introduce to you our new agency director, Edna Curry. She's just been confirmed by the Senate, so she's official," Arie Shaklar, the Deputy Director, then initiated the applause in the large computer room. "Ms. Curry, this is our central information technology oversight center. From here, we manage the agency's extensive computer network."

"Thanks everyone for such a warm welcome! It's an honor and a privilege to join your team. Please go back to your work. If you don't mind, I'll just walk around here a bit and get acquainted with some of you and the work that you do." Edna then started pacing behind many of the technicians facing their monitors.

"Hi, I'm Royce Calvey. I'm the Director of IT here. Listen, if you have any questions, please let me know."

"Thanks. So, what's going on today? Are they always this intense?"

"Actually, it is a bit of a pressure cooker right now. Not your fault. Our agency is suffering from a denial of service attack. It looks like it's originating in China."

"Oh my God! Shouldn't we call somebody?" asked Edna.

"We are that somebody. *Our* job is to maintain the computer security. It's fairly routine, but I have to admit these attacks are getting more and more common and they're actually getting better at it," Royce sighed heavily and then continued. "Even though we're not a national security agency, we do have a few links to the Pentagon and intelligence services. I suspect they're trying to distract us, while someone else is attempting to find a backdoor to one of the more sensitive servers."

Arie interjected, "Edna, these folks are really good at what they do. So, don't worry so much about this. These Chinese attacks come in waves. It'll ease off soon. They're just playing around anyway. We're their biggest customer so despite some of the popular media treatments, we're not about to have another cold war. What concerns me more is that we have an army of field agents who carry around sensitive information every day on their laptop computers. We've had a few computers stolen over the past couple of years. We suspect it's various chains of organized crime trying to get information for identity theft."

"Is there that kind of information on the laptops?" Edna asked.

"Yeah, we often have confidential information about our citizen clients . . . you know, social security numbers, birth dates, that kind of thing—even credit card numbers sometimes. It's becoming a big problem and we're way behind in coming up with effective solutions. That will be one of your challenges."

DISCUSSION QUESTIONS

1. What are the implications of the agency being "way behind" on the problem? How likely is a political appointee to "have what it takes" to handle the IT problem? What about Edna Curry? What do her reactions reveal about her level of expertise?
2. Evaluate the pros and cons of housing sensitive information with an agency that is linked to national security agencies. What reactions would you expect from citizens who learn that their information has been compromised? On what basis would the needs of the agency outweigh the interests of the citizens whose information is vulnerable to theft?
3. Critique the attitudes of Arie Shaklar and Royce Calvey. What are their unstated assumptions regarding confidential information? With respect to the laptops, how can their inability to come up with effective solutions be reconciled with their ethical responsibility to protect sensitive information?
4. Should Edna trust Arie's judgment regarding the Chinese attacks? Why or why not?

CASE 48: RECORDS CHECK

Becky was the Personnel Specialist assigned to the Parks Department. On her way to visit some hiring supervisors there, she stopped by her supervisor's office to check on an issue that had been troubling her. "When you get the chance Damon, I need to ask you about something."

"Sure, go ahead."

"You know how we get the background checks from the State Bureau of Investigation for our potential hires."

"Yes."

". . . and now one of our duties is to prescreen these so that the hiring supervisors won't be unduly biased by arrest records."

"Right, because an arrest is not a conviction," said Damon.

"Yes, and also because certain minority groups are disproportionately arrested."

"We also have policies that allow us to hire a convicted felon under certain conditions and we don't want the hiring supervisors to start out with that information because it might jaundice their decision," Damon added.

"Yeah, but I'm not going there," said Becky. "What I'm getting at is we have a set of applicants for the temporary positions in the Play in the Park program. It really is a glorified daycare so that working moms can drop off their kids while school's out for the summer."

"It's extremely popular with city council. I know the program."

"Two of these applicants have odd notations," Becky explained. "One is a deferred sentence for child molestation and the other is a suspended sentence for drug trafficking. Ultimately, neither one of these is considered to be a conviction.

I'm letting you know that I'm going to find some other excuse not to pass these two individuals along to the Parks Department. If it wasn't so unsupervised and it wasn't dealing with kids, I'd have a lot fewer qualms about this."

"This goes against policy."

"That's why I'm telling you as my supervisor. The fact is, I'm not comfortable signing off on these. So, if you feel strongly about the policy, then you should sign off on these and forward them to Parks."

"No, I think I agree with you. Let's just say that 'other candidates more fully met our needs at this time.'"

DISCUSSION QUESTIONS

1. Is it ethical to go against policy in a case like this? Which ethical principles, if any, are violated? Are there any ethical principles that could serve as a basis for Becky's actions?

2. On what legal basis would you defend Becky and Damon if applicants challenged their decisions? What is the personal risk to an official who ignores policy, particularly when doing so works to the detriment of a particular citizen's interests? Would Becky and Damon face any risks if they simply followed policy?

3. Discuss the merits and inadequacies of the personnel policy. What improvements, if any, would you suggest as steps toward striking the best balance of applicant's interests and public safety?

4. From a larger ethical perspective, should the city government be running a program for kids that is so "unsupervised" in the first place? Does its popularity with voters and the city council make a difference? Are there ways to make the program more safe without costing too much money?

Bureaucracy and Public Morality

CASE 49: THE CORRECTIONS OFFICER SELECTION VIDEO

Over half of the correctional officer cadets were leaving within six weeks after their initial assignments within the state prison system. To be assigned in the first place meant completion of a six-month training program in the academy. Each of the one hundred correctional officer cadets were paid $16 per hour during the training period and that didn't include the competitive package of health and other benefits. Anna Lippert, the Director of Public Safety, had once again appealed to the state legislature for supplemental appropriations for the state's overstretched prison system. She was successful— at least for the moment, but she knew that the Corrections Department had to do something before she came back with hat in hand for more money. The prison system already had challenges, but these personnel costs were bleeding the Corrections Department dry. State Senator Greg Fry, the chair of the powerful appropriations committee, quietly warned Anna in the hall- way outside the meeting room, "You need me. I stuck my neck out for you today, but your department better deliver. Next time I might not be so generous."

After meeting with her staff, Alan Swope from the Corrections Human Resources Division recommended that the department look into a video-based testing module.

"The research shows that a well-produced video selection system actually increases test validity, but the best part is," he paused for dramatic effect, "the candidates get a very realistic preview of the job. They get a chance to dis- cover, 'Hey, that's not for me!' and voluntarily drop out of the process before too much is invested in their selection and training."

Anna looked over at James Boyer, the Corrections Administrator. As a former FBI Agent, Anna knew that her knowledge in corrections was limited and she had learned to trust James's judgment. He shrugged, smiled, and then nodded his approval.

She turned to Alan. "Let's try it on a trial basis with the next Academy."

Alan went back to his office and charged his team with researching all the options. They finally determined that BRK Assessments had produced the best video-based testing program for correctional officer cadets. In almost all of the jurisdictions that had previously used the BRK Assessment system, turnover rates were cut in half and the remaining cadets proved to have much better performance evaluations. In addition, the assessment modules were reasonably priced and could be uploaded on PCs for distribution around the state's remote testing sites.

After full implementation, the results came in even better than their high expectations. At this early stage, turnover was nearly zero and the academy instructors said that they had the best class that they ever had. Even after their assignments to their respective prison facilities, the correctional officer cadets from this class maintained a strong commitment to their new careers and their productivity by all measurements was at an all time high.

Anna received the reports on their success in selection, training, and placement and remarked, "These numbers are almost too good to be true." In fact, the Corrections Department had reached the middle of the fiscal year and for the first time since anyone could remember, it was not scrambling to make ends meet. Anna crossed another scheduled appointment to ask the legislature for more money off her calendar.

Then the bomb dropped. First, she got a call from Senator Fry who said he was getting a lot of vicious phone calls, e-mails, and letters from his constituents about the disgusting videos they had to watch while applying to be correctional officer cadets. Next, her secretary came in and told Anna to turn on the TV. The early news was doing a story on the reaction of several citizens to "Anna Lippert's porn flicks."

"What in the heck is going on?" She called her team together and they informed her that some of the applicants became upset during their video-based test. Some of the video vignettes contained shocking scenes depicting graphic violence, extremely strong language, drug abuse, homosexual relationships, prisoners throwing feces and urine at guards, and one scene which all but showed a prisoner masturbating.

"Let's all remember now that the reason this video has been so successful is because it doesn't sugarcoat the realities behind prison walls," Alan said. "If they can't stand the heat, they shouldn't go into the kitchen—that's the whole point!"

James added, "We've been doing this test for almost a year now, and this is the first complaint I've heard. My sources tell me that this 'mass protest' is being orchestrated by an opportunistic preacher at a church near one of our prisons. Our test monitors are trained to let the applicants know what kinds of scenes the video will depict and there's a big bold warning at the beginning of the video. They can't say that they weren't warned."

Alan interjected again. "Well, maybe it's just not worth it. There is a more tame video available. The only problem is that it has a much lower validity coefficient and it's correlated with a much higher rate of turnover than what we've been experiencing with our current BRK product."

"Thanks for coming in everyone," Anna said. "I think I'll take a few more of these phone calls and watch the state's editorial pages for the next few days. I'll get back to you on my decision."

DISCUSSION QUESTIONS

1. Should Anna have more closely reviewed the video selection system? Should she have discussed it with the state's political leaders in order to gain "buy-in?"
2. Is such a video program really necessary? Is it ethical to show such disturbing material? Why or why not?
3. Are there other alternatives to the video program, such as the use of psychological testing? Is such testing ethical? Why or why not?
4. Should the news agencies have contacted Anna and informed her they were going to do a piece on the video testing program so they could get her side prior to running the story?

CASE 50: INDECENT EXPOSURE AND THE BOARD OF COSMETOLOGY

The business concept proved to be wildly popular. The first newspaper article appeared only two weeks after Jeff and Brenda opened Samson's Revenge, an innovative hair salon for gentlemen. Their gimmick was simply to create a luxury salon experience for the discriminating man. They served complimentary drinks. They strategically placed widescreen TV monitors on each wall so that the customers could catch up on the latest sports news. Best of all, patrons enjoyed having their hair styled by attractive young females in provocative lingerie. Local TV stations could not resist sending camera crews to film as much as the FCC would allow. Jeff and Brenda knew they hit the big time, especially when their store became the focus of conversation on a national radio show. Enthusiastic men traveled from miles around to be pampered at Samson's Revenge. Even haircuts starting at $75 did not shorten the lines.

Unfortunately for Jeff and Brenda, their newfound business success was not without its challenges. They received a call from one of their regular clients who asked if they had heard about the upcoming meeting of the State Board of Cosmetology. The commissioners had placed on the agenda new licensure standards that included a dress code. The proposed rules would effectively mandate that licensed hairstylists would have to wear "professionally appropriate" clothes that would, at a minimum, cover everything between the shoulders and the knees.

When TV and newspaper reporters turned up again to cover this new twist in the story, Brenda was ready. She told them, "This is silly. Our girls don't reveal anything you wouldn't see at a public swimming pool."

The spokesperson for the State Board of Cosmetology stated that the commissioners had received complaints about the business, but that the rule changes had already been under consideration for over two years.

DISCUSSION QUESTIONS

1. Should a regulatory commission assigned to oversee a licensed trade be concerned about the propriety of a particular business's marketing gimmick? What if the business concept compromised the overall reputation of the trade itself? Is there any danger of this happening in this case?
2. List three interest groups that might logically object to Jeff and Brenda's business concept. What would be the motivations behind the objections of these groups? How much influence should they have over licensed trade regulation?
3. How relevant is Brenda's claim that the girls working at her salon don't reveal anything one wouldn't see at a public swimming pool? What are the unstated assumptions reflected in that assertion?
4. Evaluate the claim that the rule changes had already been under consideration for over two years. What is the purpose in making such a claim? Could the truthfulness of this statement ever be proven or disproven? How?

CASE 51: AMERICAN GENERAL OPINES ON GAYS

"Thanks General for taking my question." Reporter Ann Foster cleared her throat and than asked, "We certainly understand the official position on gays in the military, but if I may, what is your personal opinion on the matter?"

"I am speaking for myself you understand," General Foxland replied, "but my religious upbringing leads me to conclude that homosexuality is an abomination. It's offensive and immoral and anyone who practices homosexuality is committing a sin. You know, Hollywood tries to make it no big deal, but anyone with any common sense knows in their heart that it's really a crime against nature. But once again, that's how I feel and this is not an official position. I'll do whatever the Commander in Chief sets as policy."

Within hours, Foxland heard from the President who asked for his immediate resignation.

DISCUSSION QUESTIONS

1. What would be the purpose in asking for the General's personal opinion? Is it an unfair question? To what extent is the General's opinion relevant to the issue of gays in the military? Explain your answer.
2. What advice do you have for the General? Should he have answered the question? Should he have spoken freely, or simply dodged the question? Should he seek to explain himself further in the news media? What should he do now regarding the President's request?
3. Why would the President ask for the General's resignation? What unstated assumptions, if any, are implicit? Is this action ethical? Does it show an effective leadership style? What are the likely repercussions?
4. Personal opinions aside, would openly admitting gays into the military create significant organizational problems that might compromise the military's mission? Why or why not? If so, are there managerial approaches that would mitigate potential problems? Is the challenge of handling gays in the military analogous to racially integrating the military and/or admitting women? Explain.

CASE 52: HOLLYWOOD DISCOVERY

The advance team for the Blue Prism Production Studio arrived on the scene of the State Department of Mines located on the outskirts of a suburb just west of the state capital. Executive Producer Charles Liddle exited the equipment truck and went through the entrance of the small building.

The receptionist greeted him warmly, and asked, "What can we do for you today, sir?"

"I was wondering if the director of this agency is available," Charles responded.

"Yes, sir, but he's on the telephone right now. He should be through in a few moments if you'd like to wait."

"Yes, I'd appreciate that. Would you mind if in the meantime, I just walked around your office a bit?"

"Sure, go ahead. It's your tax money at work."

"Oh thanks, except it's not my tax money. I hail from California."

"What brings you to our neck of the woods?"

"Actually, we're scouting locations for an upcoming television series."

"Ooh, that sounds exciting," the secretary gushed. "You're thinking about filming here?"

"It's certainly a possibility, but I'll need to look around a bit and of course talk with your boss." Charles then walked around the office looking and making small talk with the workers. Occasionally, he formed his hands into a rectangle simulating camera angles. Finally, the receptionist called him back up to say that the administrator was available.

"Hello, my name's Charles Liddle and I want to thank you for seeing me without notice."

"My name's Vincent Pagano." The administrator stretched out his arm for a handshake. "How can I help you?"

"As I told your receptionist, I'm part of an advance team scouting for locations for an upcoming television series. We were hoping to make an offer to use your facilities over weekends and other days that your office is not busy to film on this location. What we're looking for is authenticity. Since we're making a series about government workers, this seems to be exactly what we're looking for."

"Wow! That's a new one. I'll have to take a bit to process that." Vincent gave a close second look at his visitor. "Why'd you come way out here?"

"To be honest, your state offers several tax advantages for filming here that we just can't get back in Hollywood. We need something out of the way, with a low cost of living for our crew while they work in the area. And, we need a facility that fits our profile."

"Is it a comedy or a drama?"

"We're planning on this being a comedy, along the lines of the shows *The Office* or *Scrubs*, except instead of a business or a hospital, we would have a government agency. Like *The Office*, it would be in a 'mockumentary' style."

"The state owns the building and I am allowed to let other organizations use the facilities outside normal working hours, but we've never done anything like you're proposing here before."

"The way this would work is that we would be on site for about two weeks filming a pilot episode. We would then go into post-production and we might need to make one more visit on site for more filming. If we're happy with the outcome after editing and final production, we would then farm it out to our agents to sell to the networks. Our target audience would be one of the up-and-coming cable networks that are offering increased amounts of original programming. If we made the deal, we would then be back on site for about another fifteen weeks or so filming thirteen additional episodes. That would constitute the first mini-season. If the ratings are promising, then we'd get the go-ahead for another round. If we're lucky enough to get that far, we'd probably end up dedicating a studio to the project. So whether the show ends up being a success or not, we would probably be out of your hair within the year."

"What's in it for us?"

"We'll pay, and pay generously. In fact, we're prepared to compensate the State Department of Mines the equivalent of all payroll and overhead expenses, including utilities, for a full year. We've checked, and we know that your agency has a small budget. This should ease things up for you considerably. We've also already checked with the Governor's office, and you also have a State Filming Commission. They'll probably encourage you to allow us to film here. It might also be fun for you and your employees because we'd like to use as many of them as possible as extras. We'll pay them the standard fee for on-camera time, plus you'd get a few residuals when the show goes into reruns."

Vincent stepped back into his office and sat down at his desk. He motioned for Charles to have a seat. For a few seconds he was deep in thought. Then he finally asked, "Tell me more about the show itself."

"I hate to admit it, but it's fairly formulaic. We'd have a crusty, but benign male boss whose incompetence is masked by both his obsession with appearances and the hard work of his smarter but unrecognized subordinates. We'd have a running gag—I'm thinking rocks here. If we kept the Department of Mines theme, which is as good as anything else, we'd have the employees talking at length about rocks and rock samples, maybe even having pet rocks. We'd have an odd assortment of characters playing the office workers. An older woman who's past her prime but is still on the hunt to recreate her promiscuous past. We might have a gay guy who's still in the closet, but everybody knows his orientation. We might have a nerd who has a crush on the office cutie. You know, stuff like that. And, what would make our show unique is we could play off the stereotype of the lazy government worker."

Vincent waited a moment to respond. "You know, I'm not saying no right off the bat here, and there's no doubt that this offer is tempting. I have to tell you that I belong to a professional society that is dedicated to enhancing the image of hard-working public servants. Participating in this project sounds like I would be facilitating the very same kind of bureaucrat bashing that I've worked so hard over the years to combat. I'm just not comfortable with your proposal."

"It is a generous offer and think what you could do to advance your department's mission of mine safety. You might even save lives with these additional resources. Besides, nobody takes this stuff seriously."

Vincent looked unmoved.

Finally, Charles said, "Here, take my card. I'm also going to leave you our standard contract. Feel free to have your attorneys at the capitol take a look. I'll get back with you next week. In the meantime, feel free to give me a call if you should have any questions."

After Vincent escorted Charles out of the office, he returned inside to see his staff waiting with eager faces. Someone asked, "Is it true that we're going to be on TV?" Then they all chimed in with questions and comments.

DISCUSSION QUESTIONS

1. Are the show's producers taking any risks by partnering with an actual public sector agency? Based on your knowledge of bureaucratic pathologies, advise the producers about the potential frustrations awaiting them.
2. From the agency's perspective, what are the pitfalls of accepting revenue from a private sector entity? What conflicts of interest would be created by the partnership? In what ways would the mission of the agency be affected?
3. Is Vincent being too sensitive about the potential for bureaucrat bashing? Are these objections relevant to the decision that he must make? Assuming they are, do you think there is a corresponding possibility that the image of the agency, or the public sector generally, could be enhanced by the show? What other positive effects could accrue to the organization from the story lines that are likely to unfold?
4. If Vincent doesn't accept the deal, the production company will probably just move on to another location that's more accommodating to the show's premise. Is this reason sufficient for Vincent to agree to the proposal and have his organization enjoy the other benefits? Would it be realistic for Vincent to negotiate an adjustment in the storyline that would reflect more positively on the image of government workers?

CASE 53: ADVERTISEMENT FOR TOPLESS BAR IN UNIVERSITY NEWSPAPER

Rachel was in a quandary. She had been assigned as the new Director of Advertising for the forthcoming academic year at the student newspaper at the state university. A local bar known for its topless entertainment requested placing a help wanted ad in the paper. She took it to her editor for his opinion.

"I think we should go ahead and run it. We run advertisements for other bars. The law says they can't let in anyone under 21 anyway."

Rachel responded, "They may not be allowed to serve liquor, but this ad is asking for girls 18 years or older."

Her editor said, "They can still vote and serve in the military. They're adults. It's legal in this town. It's your decision, but I say go ahead and take their money. If the ad is provocative enough, it might even help us sell more newspapers."

"Tom, you keep forgetting that we give our newspapers away."

"Oh yeah. You know what I mean," he said. "Listen, if you're still uneasy about this, go visit Dr. Chapman and see what she says."

Dr. Christine Chapman, the faculty advisor to the student paper, came through the office later that day and Rachel presented her with the issue.

"Rachel, it's your decision and I will back you up on it. But I advise that you don't run this advertisement. I know it sounds cliché but I think topless dancing objectifies and degrades women. We should be all about uplifting the status of women. The more practical side is that approving the running of this ad might spark a giant controversy in the media or among parents or both. As representatives of this university, we act in loco parentis. They may be adults legally, but should we really be encouraging women—or men for that matter—to go into bars? I'm not even sure about our longstanding policy to allow advertisements for beer and alcohol. I don't want to sound like a prude, but maybe we should revisit that standard operating procedure."

Rachel went back to her desk even more perplexed about what she would decide.

DISCUSSION QUESTIONS

1. What are the sources of Rachel's quandary? List the conflicting values at play in her decision-making process.
2. Should Rachel simply avoid controversy by refusing to run the ad? In general, should the potential for controversy dissuade media outlets from running ads? What are the ethical implications of your answer?
3. Evaluate the arguments put forth by the editor. Does it matter that other bars are allowed to run ads? Are there any potential legal considerations? Does it matter that they are looking for girls under the age of 21?
4. Critique the advice provided by Dr. Chapman. Is it reasonable to assert that a university assumes the role of parent to girls (women?) between the ages of 18 and 21? Which ethical perspectives would help you defend the longstanding policy to allow advertisements for beer and alcohol?

Diversity Management

CASE 54: SENSITIVITY TRAINING AND PANDORA'S BOX

Kara had always had what could be described best as an eccentric personality. As her only coworker in the Personnel Testing Unit, Miguel had noticed something unusual. If he was in a good mood, Kara's quirks would be an endless source of amusement. If he was in a bad mood, those same quirks would just be plain irritating. The difference Miguel discovered was his own frame of mind. Kara was consistently a "kook" and he tried to even out his own reactions to her. They worked together in a small, confined area. One side of their office opened up to the civil service testing area and so their working space did seem bigger than its actual size.

One of her eccentricities was that she would talk to herself. Kara was a single mother of two daughters, and these one-sided conversations played out as advice she would give to her children. Other times, she'd hear something provocative on the radio and she would voice her arguments against the points of the show's host or callers. Kara's off-and-on-again boyfriend would occasionally call. Even after she hung up, the conversations might continue for several minutes. These musings were barely audible, but Miguel still had to make the effort to tune her out.

Since hiring had been picking up, Kara and Miguel were joined by Cassie who was a temporary hire. Kara may have been goofy but Miguel thought the only word to describe Cassie was moody. And it was nearly impossible to tell what mood she may be in during any given moment. Miguel was a friendly sort and if he passed Cassie in the hallway, he was sure to say hello. To his dismay, Cassie would go past without even a nod. After being ignored this way a few times, Miguel learned not to acknowledge Cassie. He thought she wouldn't notice but she soon confronted him.

"Miguel, you're being rude. We passed by each other this morning and you didn't even deign to say hello."

"I'm sorry Cassie. I must not have noticed you."

"I know you did," Cassie continued. "Next time, don't pretend you don't see me!"

That seemed to be Miguel's lot in life—always having to walk on eggshells lest he provoke Cassie's wrath.

One day, each of the three personnel technicians were working independently. Cassie was sorting through materials she received from the remote testing sites. Kara was walking back and forth sorting test booklets, and as usual, she was maintaining her constant monologue of mental musings. Miguel was doing his best to avoid interactions with either one of his coworkers when suddenly Cassie yelled.

"What did you say?"

Kara stopped her muttering and looked at Cassie.

"Oh, I didn't realize I was talking out loud. Excuse me please."

"I am a proud African American woman. I work hard. And I don't appreciate what you said," Cassie yelled back.

Miguel realized he must have missed something.

"Oh Cassie, I wasn't talking about you. I was thinking about a conversation I was having with my boyfriend," Kara explained.

"You said welfare moms should be kicked off the rolls. Just because you're white doesn't mean that you know anything about being on welfare or being black."

Kara looked puzzled. "What are you talking about? My boyfriend wants me to get food stamps to help feed my two kids. I don't think that's honorable. I didn't say anything about blacks being on welfare."

"That's what you meant and I'm going upstairs to file a grievance on you." Cassie stormed out.

Miguel's eyes met Kara's, and for a few seconds both looked dumbfounded. Then they returned to work. A half hour later, Cassie came back and sat at her desk and the three of them did not speak the rest of the day.

A week later, the agency administrator sent an e-mail to all the employees saying that everyone would be scheduled to take mandatory sensitivity training. The e-mail said that this was in response to a certain racial incident that had occurred between two employees. Training would therefore be imposed in order to prevent such episodes in the future. Miguel knew what sparked this training. He resented having to go through mandatory political correctness indoctrination just because his two coworkers could not play well with others.

Miguel thought the training would be boring but it turned out to be very stimulating. The facilitator was a professor from the state university, Dr. Johnson. He was extremely adept at getting people to open up. Dr. Johnson's goal was to uncover all the hidden conflicts. He said that before one begins to deal with these kinds of issues, one has to be aware of them. Dr. Johnson also said that one had to be aware of one's own biases and prejudices. Through a series of exercises and through extensive discussion, which at times turned extremely confrontational, the participants laid bare their souls. They dragged up grievances from long ago. Participants told how other participants had wronged them—how their feelings had been hurt by the actions and words of others. Dr. Johnson kept it going. He would proclaim in his loud, confident voice, "This is healthy. Get it out! Get it out!"

Dr. Johnson facilitated each participant to give voice to all of his or her unresolved problems with coworkers. He was very motivating in getting the agency employees to unpack their hidden hostilities. Then the training ended. The professor proved to be a master at getting the group to expose their conflicts with each other and with others. Unfortunately, he was not as adept at getting them to adequately resolve these issues once they were revealed—at least not in the time available. The result: For the next several months all the agency employees remained extremely angry with each other. Friendships were broken. Professional relationships that were productive suddenly were not. Agency turnover reached an all-time high as almost everyone tried to escape from having to face his or her colleagues on a daily basis.

Miguel may have been the most resentful of all, because when he returned to the office he shared with Kara and Cassie, they seemed absolutely oblivious that the mandatory training and the resulting turmoil had anything to do with them. Kara remained as goofy as ever. And Cassie was as moody as ever.

DISCUSSION QUESTIONS

1. Evaluate Miguel's agency in terms of personnel selection, management effectiveness, and leadership style. Which of these factors contributed most to the volatile situation in Miguel's environment? Give at least two ideas for improving organizational effectiveness in these areas.
2. What is your opinion of the sensitivity training approach to the problem? What is the logic behind requiring this training for all employees? Is mandatory sensitivity training likely to be an effective way to improve the performance of the organization? What are some other possible reasons the administrator took this approach?
3. Imagine you are a consultant brought in by top management to provide guidance in handling the new turnover problem. What advice can you offer?
4. When facing problems with particular employees, some managers prefer to generally inform the work group about a new policy to deal with the problem or to remind everyone about relevant existing policy. In terms of keeping up morale for the work group overall and ensuring adherence to work requirements, is this indirect approach a measured way to keep everyone in line with expectations? Or would it be preferable for a manager to deal more directly and immediately with those employees violating work rules?

CASE 55: THE FAIR EMPLOYMENT PRACTICES ACT

"What makes you the great expert? Are you an attorney?" Irene Mayer had given up all patience with her junior colleague, Stan Bragg. But she thought that her last question should trump any response he might make. She wanted this endless debate to end. He was wrong. Move on.

"No, I'm not an attorney," Stan responded. He deliberately tried to control his voice from rising. "But I do have a graduate education and I know how to read. Simply put, the 'Fair Employment Practices Act' is illegal. I think you're scared to have an attorney address my concern."

"Oh, come on. A hundred attorneys have addressed this law. It was written by attorneys. Who do you think makes up the state legislature?"

"Maybe so, but FEPA was written before passage of the Civil Rights Act of 1991," Stan continued. "That changed everything."

"Well, we've been overseeing the implementation of this law here in the state Office of Personnel Management for over twenty years now, and I don't remember anyone having any difficulties with how it's been implemented—before or after 1991." Irene placed some folders into her briefcase. "Anyway, I've got to run. All you need to know is that the administrator supports our current interpretation. If you keep this up, people are going to question your sensitivity to affirmative action."

"Is that a threat?"

"It's an observation."

"Maybe that's why nobody questions this law," Stan said, "because they're afraid of being labeled a racist. The real irony here is that FEPA is used to discriminate against the very minorities it's set up to help."

Irene stopped. She put her briefcase down. That was a point she hadn't heard before. "What exactly do you mean by that?"

"Could you please just take a second to go through the language of both laws and then look at how we've put FEPA into practice? If you would give me a full listen, I promise not to bring this up again—at least while you remain my supervisor."

She sighed. "All right. I'm listening." Irene sat down in her chair. Stan started pulling sheets of paper out of his files.

"Okay, here's the original FEPA law. Read it while I search online for the 1991 federal Civil Rights Act." Stan placed a sheet of paper in front of Irene before walking quickly over to a nearby computer.

Irene began to read—and not for the first time—the statutory language of the state Fair Employment Practices Act:

§74-840-4.12 (Subsection H)

1. This subsection shall be known and may be cited as the "Fair Employment Practices Act."

2. Agencies of this state may use the optional hiring procedure provided in this subsection to employ females, blacks, Hispanics, Asian/Pacific Islanders and American Indians/Alaskan natives, as defined by the Equal Employment Opportunity Commission, who are legal residents of the state in competitive and noncompetitive jobs. Individuals must meet the minimum qualifications and pass any required examinations established by the Office of Personnel Management or by statute. Except for any required examinations and minimum qualifications specified in applicable job specifications, such persons shall be exempt from the hiring procedures administered by the Office of Personnel

Management. Persons may only be employed under this subsection in a job family level, group or category which has been identified as underutilized and in which an appropriate hiring goal has been set in the state agency's affirmative action plan approved by the Office of Personnel Management pursuant to the provisions of Section 840-2.1 of this title. In addition, the appointing authority of the employing agency must determine that a manifest imbalance exists which justifies remedial action pursuant to this subsection in order to reach the affirmative action hiring goal. Provided further, that eligible war veterans, as defined by Section 67.13a of Title 72 of the State Statutes, who are members of the group for which a hiring goal has been set shall be considered by the employing agency before a nonveteran is appointed pursuant to this subsection.

3. To be eligible for appointment, the persons who are members of the group for which a hiring goal has been set must score within the top ten scores of other available members of said group based on any examination or rating of education and experience.

"All right I'm finished," Irene said.

"Okay, hold on," Stan waited for the fruits of his search to print. "Now look at this."

Irene took the paper, still warm from the printer, and started to read. Then she stopped. "This goes on for pages. I don't have time for this."

"Okay," Stan said, "Then before you go, please describe to me, as briefly as you would like, how we actually implement FEPA here at the state OPM."

"As you already know," Irene said patiently, "the hiring agency sends OPM a personnel requisition for the position they wish to make a hire. We approve it based on budget considerations and whatever other policy is in effect at the time. When they get our approval, they can then pull a register of eligible applicants from the state roster. If their particular agency or department has underutilized a particular minority, they can pull from the list of eligibles the top scores of only those qualified applicants that are from that minority."

"Or females as the case may be," reminded Stan.

"Right, or females if they have a manifest imbalance in terms of gender for their particular hiring effort."

"So in other words," Stan said, "an agency can—in accordance with the hiring goals of its affirmative action plan—pull a register that is exclusively of one minority or another."

"That is correct."

"For example," Stan offered, "let's assume that the Department of Corrections has a hundred correctional officers in its flagship prison. Out of that hundred, only two correctional officers are African American. The available workforce for African Americans in that job category suggests that there should be about ten percent actually hired. Therefore, that job classification is underutilized in reference to African Americans."

"I'm with you," Irene said.

"So, under FEPA, the Corrections Department can request a certificate of only African Americans."

"That's right."

"But what if Hispanics are also underutilized? Can the agency still just pull a list of African Americans?"

"Well, yes," Irene said, "but they also can pull a list of Hispanics later on if necessary."

"In any case, the agency can draw a list of eligible names exclusively in favor of one minority at the expense of all other minorities and even white males."

"Yes, that's what's been done."

"You don't see anything wrong in that?"

"No. The FEPA registers have performed an incredible service over the years in ensuring that the state's workforce represents the diversity of its citizens."

"I may not be an attorney; but if I were, I'd hate to have to defend the state against an African American female who made the highest score on the competitive examination, but whose name was never pulled on a certificate of eligibles just because an agency had arbitrarily decided to pull a FEPA certificate of a different minority."

"Is that all you got?" Irene asked dismissively.

"Actually, no. That wasn't my real point at all." Stan directed Irene's attention to the paper in front of her. "Look down at Section 106 of the Civil Rights Act of 1991." He pointed down about midway through the fifth page. Read that language right there."

Irene focused her eyes on the following language of the federal Civil Rights Act:

Section 106. Prohibition Against Discriminatory Use of Test Scores.

(1) It shall be an unlawful employment practice for a respondent, in connection with the selection or referral of applicants or candidates for employment or promotion, to adjust the scores of, use different cutoff scores for, or otherwise alter the results of, employment related tests on the basis of race, color, religion, sex or national origin.

Irene was exasperated. "That's not relevant. That's the language that forbids race norming."

"And what exactly is race norming?"

"Like it says here, race norming is adjusting scores or using differential passing points on tests based on a person's demographic status in terms of race and gender," Irene responded. "We don't do either. The scores stay exactly the same on the FEPA list. And they still have to pass the competitive exam just like every other candidate."

"I would argue that the FEPA certificate is the ultimate result of the competitive testing process," Stan said. "Would you agree?"

"I guess so."

"Then you have basically made my point. The FEPA certificate violates the Civil Rights Act of 1991 because it has systematically created de facto cut-off scores that are different from one minority to the next."

"I think you're stretching this a bit far."

"Am I?" Stan pointed once again to the text. "See here. It says 'or otherwise alter the results of . . . employment related tests on the basis of race, color, religion, sex or national origin.' That's exactly what the FEPA does."

"I still don't buy it."

"Do you even see my point?"

"I think so, but it is so weak."

"If I can make you see my point, I bet a creative attorney can really make a jury see the point, especially in this conservative state." Stan paused for effect. "All that I'm asking is that we make an appointment with the agency administrator and bring these issues up before we get blindsided by a long-overdue lawsuit. Whether or not anybody sues or not, I think the reason why no one is upset is that no one understands the intricacies of our hiring process. If the veterans groups got wind of how we've implemented FEPA, they would go nuts. Despite what the state law says, unless they're a member of a minority, it throws their veterans' preference right out the window."

"I'll see if I can get us on his schedule," Irene said, "but be aware, that I'm not taking your side. If it weren't for the FEPA registers, too many of our state agencies would still be reserved for the good ol' boys."

"That's fair. Thanks for letting me have my say."

DISCUSSION QUESTIONS

1. Beyond the question of legality, is the Fair Employment Practices Act an ethical law? Why or why not? Is there a distinction between the law itself and how it's implemented?
2. Should race ever be considered in hiring? If so, how can a more fair system be developed? Is it possible to create a system that treats race as one of many factors considered, or is that too subjective?
3. Is Stan a racist? Explain your answer.
4. Do minorities still suffer discrimination in today's workplace? Has the election of an African American to the White House helped the United States enter into a "post-racial" era? As a public administrator, what workplace policies, if any, would you consider to encourage and manage diversity in your organization?

CASE 56: WEEKEND RACIST

Angie almost deleted the e-mail. She wondered why the spam filter hadn't caught this one since the subject line read, "ALERT: Carl is a Racist!" But then she noticed the e-mail came from another agency employee. Also, among Angie's many other duties, she supervised the mail room and the postal clerk there. Hesitantly, she opened the e-mail and there was a note from Lisa, an African American accounting clerk in another division. It said simply: "Carl in the mail room is a racist. He is a member of a local hate group. Click on this link and you will see how he spends his weekends. Angie still wasn't sure that this wasn't some scam. After all, the spammers could be quite clever. But she was intrigued. Hesitantly, she connected to the link. It was a page full of thumbnail photographs. They were so small that she couldn't quite make out any of them. So she put her cursor over one and clicked. There was Carl, the postal clerk, in full paramilitary regalia. On his right arm, he wore an armband with a Nazi swastika. In the background, he was flanked by an array of photographs of cross burnings and lynchings. From the ceiling hung three confederate flags. The other pictures were just as damning. She immediately called Carl into her office and asked him what this was all about. He said, "Excuse me Angie, but what I do on my own time is my business. We have fun and we never do anything illegal."

"I don't think so," Angie responded, "We must have some moral turpitude clause or something that might even get you fired."

"I wouldn't go there." Carl stiffened and lowered his eyes. "Every one of my performance appraisals have been superior. It would be advisable for you to drop this matter right now."

"Are you threatening me?"

"I am going back to the mail room to do my job. I suggest you do the same rather than wasting your time playing on the Web." At that Carl turned and left the room.

Angie was stunned. She got up and headed down the hall to see if the agency administrator was in her office. Lisa stopped her on the way and asked, "Did you get my e-mail?"

"Yes, I'm still looking into it."

"I want that bigot fired, Angie," yelled Lisa. Several other employees peeked from around their cubicles.

"We'll see," Angie said. She continued down the hall away from Lisa. Angie did not know what she would recommend to the administrator.

DISCUSSION QUESTIONS

1. Should Angie begin termination proceedings against Carl? Why or why not? Is a public employee's free time of no concern to the agency that hired him or her? Does your answer depend on the position that the employee holds? If, for example, Carl was a police officer, would your answer change? Why or why not? What about illegal drug use? Would your answer to this question be different if Carl was a social drug user rather than a racist? Why or why not?

2. How should we resolve our commitments to conflicting values? Equality is espoused in the Declaration of Independence as a core American value and guaranteed in the 14th Amendment of the U.S. Constitution; however, the freedom of association is also guaranteed by the First Amendment. How would you rank or order these sometimes competing values?

3. Did Lisa act ethically in this situation? Does she have the "right" to demand that Carl be fired? Did she act ethically in creating a scene in the hall? Explain your answer.
4. Before taking any action against Carl, should the agency consider the potential cost of litigation that might be involved in a civil rights action? Why or why not?

CASE 57: ACCOMMODATING A STUDENT WITH A DISABILITY

After passage of the American's with Disabilities Act (ADA) in 1990, the University of Central Arkansas hired Lance Haffner as Director of the University's Office of Disability Compliance. Lance's job was to process and implement accommodations for students, faculty, and staff with disabilities. Since to a certain extent each individual with a disability is unique, Lance was given broad discretion in developing and implementing accommodations for individuals with disabilities at the university. However, with regard to making accommodations in academic programs, individual professors and departments had the final word on whether an accommodation would be granted.

Shortly after being hired, Lance received a phone call from Cameron Miller, a new freshman at the University, who requested a meeting with Lance to discuss accommodations for his disability. Lance scheduled an appointment for Monday of the following week.

When Cameron arrived at Lance's office, he was in a wheelchair, and he told Lance that he suffered from a condition known as dystonia.

Lance told Cameron, "I have never heard of that condition before. Could you please tell me a little about your condition?"

"Well, dystonia is a neurological movement disorder. It causes involuntary muscle spasms which can force parts of the body into painful and often abnormal movements or positions. It can affect any part of the body. In my case, it currently affects my arms, legs, and sometimes my eyelids and vocal cords," replied Cameron as he handed Lance a thick file of documentation from his neurologist.

"I see," said Lance. "So, what types of accommodations do you think you are going to need?"

"As a result of my condition, I take a lot of medication, some of which makes me very drowsy. So, in high school I was exempt from any attendance requirements. Also, I was allowed to take home all assignments and tests because when my condition is acting up it can take me a long time to complete a test or project."

"I don't think that making modifications to any attendance policy your professors might have will be a problem, but I am going to get a lot of resistance to allowing you to have take-home exams. I don't think that most people on the faculty here are going to be very receptive to that idea, and I don't really have the power to force a professor to grant that request. I am not sure that such a request is even reasonable given our obligation to protect the integrity of our academic programs."

Cameron became visibly upset and retorted, "Under the ADA, you have to give me what I want. It's not fair that I have this condition. In order for me to be successful in school, these are the things I need. It's all there in my documentation. I can't pass unless I get take-home tests. I become exhausted and have to rest as a result of the pain and the medication. Unless I pass and stay in school, I can't stay on my parents' insurance. How in the heck am I supposed to be able to afford all the medications I have to take without insurance?"

"Believe me I am very sympathetic to your position, Cameron, but I just don't think that take-home tests are a reasonable accommodation under the ADA. What if we allowed you to have extended time, and let you take the tests in our testing center where you could rest if you needed too? That would allow us to monitor the tests and ensure their integrity."

"That's not good enough," replied Cameron. "I have to lie down sometimes when I get tired, and besides, I need the tests to be open book, because I suffer from short-term memory loss due to some of the drugs I have to take."

"I am just not sure that is going to be possible, Cameron."

"Look! I know my rights, and I have a lawyer. If you don't accommodate me, this whole thing could get messy and costly for this university."

"Okay, Cameron. I will see what we can do, but I am going to need to talk to my boss about this. I will give you a call in the next couple of days," Lance replied.

DISCUSSION QUESTIONS

1. Should Lance ask Cameron's professors to grant his requested accommodations? Are Cameron's accommodations reasonable?
2. Given the fact that universities don't have unlimited funds, should Lance take Cameron's threat of costly litigation into consideration when evaluating his requested accommodations? Is it ethical for Cameron to threaten litigation in order to pressure Lance into granting his accommodation requests?
3. Should Lance consider that Cameron's health might be affected by his decision if he didn't grant the accommodations and Cameron was not able to maintain health insurance as a result? What ethical theory can be cited in support of granting this request? What theory can be cited to oppose such a request?
4. Should the fact that Cameron was given take-home tests in high school be considered, or should a college be more stringent in its requirements? If Cameron's accommodations are granted, is that fair to other students who don't get open-book or take-home tests?

CASE 58: HATE SPEECH IN CONFIDENTIAL COURSE EVALUATIONS

"You are understandably upset about this, but I assure you that we will find the culprit." said Penny Barrett, the Dean of the College of Liberal Arts. "Such inflammatory language has no place at this university. I've already talked with the president of the university and the legal office. We're going to hire both a handwriting expert and a private detective to investigate the matter. I promise you that we will find the culprit who used the "n" word on this course evaluation."

"I am upset," said Professor Becker. "You'd think in this day and age when we can have an African American as president of the United States and minorities as CEOs of major corporations that we'd be past this. I have to ask, how can you get around the fact that we tell our students that these are anonymous course evaluations."

"We've already discussed that and as you know, this university has a policy against hate speech. I think that policy will supercede any promise of anonymity. You need to understand that this isn't just about you. This kind of language is an attack on every academician of color and we can't just let these comments stand. They're not made in good faith to provide you feedback about your course or your teaching style."

DISCUSSION QUESTIONS

1. Evaluate Barnett's assertion that the integrity of the process is subordinate to the hate speech policy. Is this based on an ethical principle, a managerial objective, a legal issue, or what?

2. Advise the university's Public Relations Department about what they should expect regarding this matter. Should any effort be made to keep this out of the press? Or, should it be publicized for some reason? What is your prediction regarding public opinion on the hate speech and the way the university is handling the situation?

3. Discuss Professor Becker's reaction to the use of the "n" word. Does the word carry the same connotations today as in the past? What are the cultural, generational, or perhaps class differences in how words like this are interpreted?

4. If you were the administrator in charge of this situation, how would you handle the student who filled out the course evaluation if his or her name became known to you? Is this a relatively minor infraction or is it serious enough to warrant dismissing this student from the university? Explain your answer.

CASE 59: EQUAL PAY EXPERTS IN A HOT TUB

Merit Protection Arbitrator Dallas Dalton had finally had enough. For the umpteenth time, he had sat there and listened to the testimony of competing "expert" witnesses. In this case, the controversy centered on Department of Transportation (DOT) director, Willoughby Ward Tompkins.

Testifying on behalf of eight female DOT managers, statistician Sid Iona maintained that Tompkins was exhibiting gender bias in terms of pay, with females making 82 percent of what men in similar positions were paid. "Therefore," according to Iona, "these figures clearly indicate the need for compensation adjustments." With this, Martin Hadley, the attorney for the female employees, concluded his questioning of Iona.

But his counterpart, Buckley Stanhope, countered with another expert, Dr. Filbert Nuxhall. Dr. Nuxhall had testified at more than two dozen hearings, each time armed with conclusions that aided DOT's case.

"Looking into these data at a deeper level," said Dr. Nuxhall, "reveals a real problem with regard to comparability. In fact, there is not a single case where we can compare two employees as being 'equal' in terms of work performed, experience, and effectiveness of performance. It is overly simplistic to compare pay rates on the basis of gender groupings alone, because at the managerial level no two jobs are very much alike."

"Enough!" exclaimed Dalton. The room fell silent as all eyes turned to the arbitrator. "I have had it with you so-called 'expert' witnesses. If it is not obvious to everyone in this room already, I am saying right here and now in front of everyone that these witnesses are no better than prostitutes. No offense to Dr. Nuxhall and Iona, but they get paid, probably more than a thousand bucks each, to say whatever they can to persuade you to their client's argument. I for one would actually like to know whether we can objectively discuss the pay issues at stake here. Apparently, we won't get very far toward that goal in a proceeding like this. In my opinion, being an expert witness for a living is not honest work. Personally, I would need a long, hot shower after testifying."

The attorneys and their clients were stunned beyond words at Dalton's outburst. They simply froze, wondering what would happen next. Then Dalton held up a piece of paper and waved it above his head, addressing the two attorneys.

"Do you fellas know what this is?" he asked, waving the paper in the direction of Stanhope and Hadley. "I will tell you what it is, and I am passing copies to each of you. It's from a Web site originating in Queensland, Australia," he continued. "They've had enough of these dog and pony shows down there. No more 'expert testimony for hire' in Queensland. They've got this new thing called 'hot-tubbing,' and I am going to try it out here. You can file all the objections you want, because this case is headed for an Equal Employment Opportunity Commission appeal anyhow." As Dalton reached for his gavel, the attorneys began to read their copies. "I am ordering a recess until noon tomorrow."

The two attorneys were already familiar with the "hot-tubbing" methodology being practiced in Australia. This is a process where expert witnesses are examined and cross-examined in a manner that is different from the way other witnesses testify at a hearing. Specifically, the expert witnesses for *both* sides are put on the stand as a group, or a "panel," to offer testimony. During that phase of the proceeding, protocol is more relaxed, with discussions back and forth among the experts, attorneys, and the arbitrator. When this method is used in a court of law, the experts testify together at the trial, discussing the case, asking each other questions, and in general making an honest effort at finding common ground on the important issues. In theory, this is supposed to be a better way to get at the real truth.

DISCUSSION QUESTIONS

1. Under current equal employment rules, who gains the advantage from an "expert-for-hire" contest involving a case like this one—Hadley or Stanhope? In what kind of situation would the advantage go the other way? Are adversarial expert witnesses equally appropriate in all types of cases? Discuss Dalton's criticisms of hired experts. Is his name-calling warranted? What incentives, if any, are currently in place to promote objective, unbiased testimony? Thinking about a full-blown trial, how would members of a jury deal with opposite conclusions from two experts who appear to have equally lofty credentials? What are the implications of this?

2. Critique the behavior of Hadley and Stanhope. Are they undermining the pursuit of fairness by using Iona and Dr. Nuxhall? Would they and their fellow attorneys be likely to welcome the "hot-tubbing" methodology? Why would they? Why wouldn't they?

3. According to one legal scholar, two assumptions underlie the hot-tubbing approach—judges who really are interested in ferreting out the truth, and experts who are candid. How realistic are these assumptions? What are some other ways to make the adversarial process a little less adversarial when it comes to expert testimony?

4. Would hot-tubbing be a good method for public administrators to use in other aspects of their decision making? Why or why not?

Challenges in Nonprofit Management

CASE 60: FIREFIGHTERS GET MONEY FOR CHARITY

The hospital triage nurse called his cell phone with alarming news. The 11-year-old girl who had been Dr. Markey's patient for the last two months was now in intensive care. The good doctor realized he needed to hurry. Thankfully, the light ahead had just turned green. Dr. Markey sped up to make sure he got through the intersection before the light turned yellow. Just then, the solitary figure standing just off the road stepped into Dr. Markey's lane. He slammed on his brakes. The antilock system engaged, but still he could not stop in time. He swerved his car off the road. His Lexus hopped the curb and the front of his car rammed underneath the concrete bench at the bus stop. Dr. Markey felt as if someone had punched him in his stomach and face at the same time. Slowly he gained awareness of his surroundings. His airbag had deployed. Dr. Markey couldn't see anything, but he could hear voices all around him.

The voice to his immediate left said, "Stay still." Dr. Markey obeyed. He heard the voice yell, "Does anybody have a crow bar?" Shortly afterward, Dr. Markey heard the crunching of metal beside him. He looked up and saw a firefighter. How did he get here so fast?

"How long have I been unconscious?"

"I'm not sure you have. You've just been in an accident."

"I realize that, but how long have I been out?" Dr. Markey received no response. "How long ago did the accident happen?"

"Just now . . . a few seconds ago," said the firefighter. "Lucky for you, I was already here. We're calling for an ambulance now. I'm going to need to remove some of these obstructions."

Dr. Markey suddenly realized that the firefighter was the person he was trying to avoid hitting. "You were the one in the street."

"Yeah, I'm out collecting money for the annual In the Boot Charity for the kids."

The mention of children sparked Dr. Markey's memory. "Oh, I just remembered. I need someone to call county hospital."

"We're going to take you over to St. John's. It's a lot closer."

"No, no. You don't understand. Call the county hospital. I've got a patient in critical care waiting for me. Tell them that Dr. Markey has been detained and they have to proceed without me." A police car arrived on the scene and an officer jumped out. The firefighter told the officer to contact the county hospital with Dr. Markey's message.

Later, as the paramedics were transporting Dr. Markey to the ambulance, the officer caught up to him and asked what happened.

"Well, I was in a hurry, but I don't think I was speeding. That firefighter who helped me was walking on the side of the road and for no apparent reason walked into my lane. He was not in the crosswalk. I tried to stop, but couldn't. I made a sharp turn away and ended up in the bus stop. Thank God there was nobody waiting for a bus at the time."

"So, you're telling me that the firefighter inexplicably walked right out in front of you."

"Well, he told me he's doing that charity work where they go around to different cars and have the drivers put money in their boot."

DISCUSSION QUESTIONS

1. Should Dr. Markey be ticketed for any traffic offenses? Did Dr. Markey's decision to speed up violate any ethical principles? What ethical perspectives might be cited in defense of his decision to speed up?
2. Should the firefighter face any civil or criminal penalties? Is he a hero in this case?
3. Millions of dollars each year are raised for charitable causes in this kind of initiative conducted by firefighters. Are the benefits outweighed by the risks?
4. If firefighters are able to raise so much money approaching cars in intersections for donations, should civilians be encouraged to engage in this style of fundraising as well? Why or why not?

CASE 61: GHOST WORKER AT THE NONPROFIT

The Texas Citizen Advocates for Recovery and Treatment Association is a 501(c)(3) nonprofit organization that receives most of its funding from the Texas Department of Health and Human Services. Seventy-five percent of the association's annual budget is provided by the state of Texas and the association's mission is to provide no-cost or discounted treatment for individuals with drug and alcohol addictions. The remaining 25 percent of the association's budget comes from client fees and private donations. Because the association receives state monies, it is subject to the state's open records requirements and is required to submit quarterly financial disclosures and reports to the Department of Health and Human Services and to the State Auditor's office.

In July, Betty Bauer was contacted by Craig Brown, the Deputy Commissioner for Mental Health at the Department of Health and Human Services. Prior to becoming Deputy Commissioner, Craig had served for sixteen years in Texas State Senate. Craig asked Betty if she might have any open positions at her organization.

Betty responded, "No Craig, right now we are completely staffed, and our budget is really tight. Why do you ask?"

"Well, a friend of mine named Jim Reynolds is looking for a job. Jim has served as the Texas State Senate's Sergeant-at-Arms for the past twenty years, and he is looking to retire from that position, but he will need to supplement his state retirement in order to make ends meet. I think that Jim could be a real asset to your organization and with his contacts in the legislature he might really be a valuable resource with things like funding issues," replied Craig.

"Well, I really wish I could help you out, Craig, but like I said our budget is tight and I don't have any openings. Besides, wouldn't it be unethical for Jim to lobby legislators after such a short period of separation from the Senate?"

Craig responded, "I don't think it would be unethical for Jim to work on your behalf. He didn't have any legislative decision-making power in his role with the state. Regarding your budget issue, I might be able to help you out if you could help me out on this deal."

"Well, let me think about it, and see what I can come up with," Betty said.

After two weeks, Craig called Betty again to see if she would hire Jim. When Betty said, that she still didn't have enough money or a position he could fill, Craig said, "I want to see your financials because I think we're looking at mismanagement here."

Faced with the prospect of an official inquiry by her primary funding source, Betty relented and hired Jim Reynolds as a business and economic development analyst and consultant. Jim's job was supposed to be to help the association develop new revenue outlets, increase private donations, and seek foundation grant monies.

After several months, Jim stopped going to his office at the association on a regular basis, and he had not increased private donations or grants at all. Betty made several inquires and requested regular updates and reports from Jim regarding his activities. However, no reports were ever produced and Betty's requests went unanswered.

Betty later learned that Jim had not resigned his post as Chief Sergeant-at-Arms for the state senate and was continuing to draw a state salary of $45,000 a year. Betty then decided to confront Jim face to face the next time he did actually come into the association's offices.

A week later, Jim came in to check his messages and Betty stopped him and said, "Jim, where are those reports I have been asking about? I need to know what kind of progress you are making."

"I know I haven't given those to you Betty, but I have been working on a number of prospects. In fact, I have just written a grant proposal for $50,000 from the Ghezzi Foundation. I have a copy of the grant right here. I was going to forward a copy to you. In addition, I have been in contact with a number of potential big donors."

Betty then inquired about Jim's other job, "I understand that you didn't resign your post with the State Senate. Do you really have time to do both jobs?"

"Well, the legislative session is only every other year, and I did go on part-time basis with the senate, so I think I can handle both jobs. I really have been out there following leads and researching grants. You know, Betty, it does take some time to develop relationships and see results when it comes to raising funds, and I have only been here five or six months," replied Jim.

Based on her conversation with Jim, Betty decided the take-a-wait-and-see approach and give Jim a few more months to develop the position and produce some tangible results.

DISCUSSION QUESTIONS

1. Should the state outsource these types of services, or should the state maintain its own treatment facilities? What would be the costs and benefits to the state by maintaining its own addiction treatment facilities? What are the advantages of outsourcing such facilities and programs? Can outsourcing lead to a type of back-door patronage system that would be prohibited by a state's merit-protection system? What types of controls might be developed to prevent this from happening?
2. Should Betty Bauer have resisted the political pressure from Craig Brown and refused to hire Jim Reynolds? Explain your answer. Should Betty have reported Craig's threat to the State's Auditor or Attorney General? Why or why not?
3. Is it ethical for a former state employee to lobby on behalf of a private entity? Should state employees have the same First Amendment rights as every other citizen when it comes to lobbying? What ethical theory would support allowing such an arrangement? What ethical theory can be cited to oppose such lobbying?
4. Should former legislators be allowed to seek and gain employment in state agencies once they leave the legislature? Why or why not? If they should be able to gain state employment, should there be a time limit after they leave the legislature before they are eligible for such employment? If the answer to the preceding questions is yes, what would be a reasonable time for a legislator to be barred from such employment?

CASE 62: SHARING THE DONOR LIST

Toward the end of the quarterly conference call, Barbara Maw, Chair of the Finance Committee for the Lindbloom County Community Action Agency (LCCAA), moved to the next agenda item, a request from the Family Planning Advocacy Group for access to LCCAA's list of donors and program participants. As a long-time sponsor of LCCAA events and programs, the Family Planning Advocacy Group was an important ally. In addition to helping with the coordination of community-wide events, the two organizations also teamed on projects to deliver social services and emergency assistance to impoverished and otherwise distressed people in Lindbloom County.

"What do we think of this request?" asked Barbara as she opened up the discussion.

Mike Jarvis spoke first. "Well, this is a no-brainer. The Family Planning Advocacy Group is one of our most important partners. They're part of a national organization. How could we possibly refuse the request?"

Then Cathy Wiregrass interjected. "I don't know, Mike. There may be a downside to this. No one would argue about how important they are to us, but this request is kind of pushy if you ask me. Barb, have they said why they want the list?"

"Not specifically, Cathy," replied Barb. "But Pam Schrader, the director over there, has told me on several occasions that they were trying to step up their fundraising efforts. I guess this would beef up their mailing list."

"And what could be wrong with that?" asked Mike. "Maybe someday we will want to have their list. And besides, we sure don't want to lose their trust and support over a simple request."

"I understand what you're saying, Mike," said Cathy. "But our donors are important to us also—not to mention the folks who use our programs and services. Now I would guess that most of them would have no objection to having their contact information provided to the Family Planning Advocacy Group, but maybe some of them wouldn't appreciate it. With its strong stand protecting abortion rights, the Family Planning Advocacy Group is a controversial organization, to say the least."

"Can I chime in?" asked Darryl Boyce, the senior member of the Finance Committee. "First of all, we make no promises to anyone that we won't share our mailing lists. I can't remember ever having done this before, but I know that other agencies share theirs. I doubt that there is any expectation among our donors that we are committed to keeping their information to ourselves. On the other hand, Cathy has a point too. Since this has never come up before, we are definitely in a gray area. We don't want to make enemies over this."

DISCUSSION QUESTIONS

1. What other possible uses could the Family Planning Advocacy Group have in mind? Should Barbara get some clarification from Pam Schrader before the committee proceeds? Which uses would be acceptable, in your opinion? Why?
2. What objections might donors have to LCCAA sharing their information with the Family Planning Advocacy Group, or just sharing the information in general? What about the program participants? Are they as likely to object as the donors? What might their objections be?
3. What expectations would you have regarding the transfer of your contact information among various nonprofit organizations? What standards or procedures would you recommend nonprofits follow when deciding issues like this? Should there be a policy for handling such requests, or should they be handled on a case-by-case basis?
4. What would you suggest to the Finance Committee regarding the Family Planning Advocacy Group's request? How would that affect LCCAA's relationship with the Family Planning Advocacy Group and other partnering organizations? How would that affect LCCAA's relationships with donors and program participants?

CASE 63: UNIVERSITY PRESIDENT PROTESTS FOOTBALL OFFICIAL'S DECISION

Stanton University President Mike Bollen could not believe his eyes. The field officials just awarded the opposing team possession of an onside kick and the decision was upheld by the replay officials in the booth. The call was clearly wrong and allowed the opposing team to win the game by one point, 34–33. Bollen could not imagine what the officials in the booth were thinking.

Within minutes of the end of the game, sport commentators were saying the same thing. Stanton fans began posting blogs and demanding that the officials be held accountable. The bad call could very well have cost Stanton University the opportunity to play in a bowl game this year. Stanton Head Coach Rob Stone held a press conference and demanded that the National Collegiate Athletic Association (NCAA) do something about this situation.

When the NCAA did not respond to Stone's press conference, Bollen decided to take matters into his own hands and spent 6 hours researching and drafting a letter to Conference Commissioner Kent Weinstein that read in part, "The lapses that occurred in last week's football game certainly constitute an outrageous injustice! Officiating is a conference responsibility, and therefore, we must look to you for justice, to right this wrong. I am requesting that you as commissioner declare last week's game a 'no game' so that it does not go into the record books for either team. It is sad that the members of our football team have been deprived of a win that they so obviously deserved because of an inexcusable breakdown in officiating."

Commissioner Weinstein responded by placing the officials on a two-game suspension, but said that nothing in NCAA rules allowed for him to void the results of a game based on bad officiating.

DISCUSSION QUESTIONS

1. If you were Commissioner Weinstein, what would you do and why?
2. Should the NCAA change its rules to allow conference commissioners to void the results of games due to bad officiating?
3. Did President Bollen overreact? Does the outcome of a football game really have moral import? College presidents are usually highly paid. Suppose that President Bollen's annual salary is $500,000 which equates to $240 an hour. Was Bollen's time well spent on this matter?
4. Would President Bollen have been as upset if the university's star debate team lost a tournament due to similarly bad officiating? Why or why not?

CASE 64: THE LAZY VOLUNTEER

Megan Shilling, star pitcher for Glenview Elementary Blue Birds, waited patiently in line for a hot dog and sports drink. Right behind her was Jarrod Blake, the best hitter on the Brook Hollow Hammers.

"Why is it taking so long, bird brain?" Jarrod asked as he slapped Megan on the back of her head. Megan slapped him back.

"Stop it Jar-head," she replied. "You just wait your turn like everybody else. They've got Mr. Bailey running the concession stand now, so don't get your hopes up. We'll be here a while."

"Old man Bailey?" Jarrod laughed. "What a joke!" Just then Jarrod's mother, Jenny, joined them in line, along with Megan's dad, Steve Shilling, the Little League Director for the Rotary Club.

"You kids get back to the field," Jenny commanded. "Mr. Shilling and I will get your drinks."

"It's good to see you, Jenny," said Steve. "It looks like there are more people in line than at the diamonds."

"I was just going to say that," Jenny replied. "This line is standing still, isn't it? Why is Mr. Bailey working back there? He must be ninety years old."

"Well, Jenny," said Steve, "it's kind of a weird story; but actually Old Man Bailey isn't the problem. He's doing the best he can, and he's still pretty good on his feet. The one slowing things down is Zachary Jones, his new 'volunteer' helper." Jenny was shocked to hear this.

"Oh my God!" she exclaimed. "Zach Jones? When did he get back from the juvenile center?"

"Last week, Jenny. Just in time for Little League season. A group of us down at the Rotary were able to get him released by promising to keep him working for the summer. Mr. Bailey was gracious enough to let Zach be his volunteer at the concession stand."

"I had no idea," Jenny replied. "That is awfully nice of Mr. Bailey. But isn't that kind of dangerous, considering Zach's temperament?"

"I suppose we'll just wait and see," answered Steve. "He's on medication and seems to be very calm. The trouble is he doesn't care one bit about keeping this line moving. It really puts Mr. Bailey in a bind, because the parents have been complaining a lot."

"Well, of course they would, Steve. Apart from the threat of Zach acting up again, there is the issue of the concession stand. It is an important part of the Little League experience, and these parents pay good money for this program. Bill and I pay over two hundred dollars for Jarrod, Mickey, and Rudy to play. I think parents have a right to expect some minimum standards in return for those fees."

"Of course, we do, Jenny," Steve acknowledged. "Believe me, I have run afoul of these parents before, and hope to never go there again. But I can tell we are going to hear about this issue loud and clear at the next Rotary Club meeting."

DISCUSSION QUESTIONS

1. What conflicts of interest are apparent in the story? What could Mr. Bailey do to address his challenges at the concession stand? What are Steve Shilling's options in handling the situation? How does funding figure into the range of options?

2. How would you characterize the position of the parents regarding the fees they pay? Does the fact that they pay to participate mean that they are "customers" of the Rotary Club? How should the Rotary Club view the parents—as customers, as beneficiaries of a generous program, as supportive community members, or something else?

3. What does the relationship between the parents and the Rotary imply about performance standards for concession stand volunteers? Is it inappropriate to impose performance standards on volunteers? What can be done about poorly performing volunteers?

4. List at least four complaints you would expect to hear at the next Rotary Club meeting. What options are available for parents who are dissatisfied with the situation? What should be done about Zach?

Environmental Protection

CASE 65: AN OMBUDSMAN BY ANY OTHER NAME

The Natural Resources Conservation Commission was created to protect the environment in the state. Provision 113 of the enabling legislation mandates that the Commission is charged with the duty to remediate hazardous waste sites in the state. Provision 113 also provides that there "shall be no pre-remediation judicial review of the agency's site plans." The result of the provision is that if the Commission makes a mistake, the public has to wait until the damage has been done to seek judicial relief. As a result of Provision 113, the legislature created a "safety valve" by amending the act to allow the Commission to create an independent Office of the Ombudsman.

In response to the amendment, the Commission promulgated Rule 2010 that established the office and detailed the duties of the ombudsman. The ombudsman's duty is to field complaints filed by citizens concerning the Commission's site remediation plans. The ombudsman is empowered to investigate complaints, site plans, and issue a public report.

Mary Flick filed one such complaint against a proposed remediation plan on an abandoned chemical plant in Greer County. The Commission's plan was to establish an incinerator site and burn 245,000 tons of toxic sludge left behind in a pit on the property by the defunct chemical company. When the plan was released, Mary became concerned and began to research toxic material incineration. Normally, this type of remediation is perfectly safe if conducted in a rural or sparsely populated area, and provided there is no mercury in the material to be incinerated. Mercury cannot be destroyed by incineration. When mercury is burned, it changes from a liquid to a gas. The gas is highly toxic and there are no safe filters that can be used on an incinerator to ensure the gas does not escape.

The Commission's remediation plan claimed that no mercury was present at the plant. However, based on court records and a state open records request, Mary discovered the presence of mercury on the site and in the pit. In addition, the incineration would be conducted in an area of 70,000 people, with a hospital and school nearby.

With the incinerator plan ten days from operation, the ombudsman, Roberto Martinez, issued a report. The report was highly critical of the Commission's site investigation, and noted a long list of potential hazards created by the proposed remediation, including the potential for severe birth defects among children born in the area, spontaneous abortions, unusually high cancer rates, and heart disease.

The Commission's Executive Director, Kristy Whitmore, was highly embarrassed by the release of the report. As a result, Kristy proposed rulemaking that would move the ombudsman's office under the supervision of the Commission's Solicitor General or legal counsel. The commission agreed and began the rulemaking process that ended with the transfer of the ombudsman to the Office of the Solicitor General. The transfer placed the ombudsman under the direct control of the agency's chief legal officer.

Roberto was told he could keep his job, but that he would have to report to the Solicitor General. Roberto resigned saying, "I would not accede to working in the Solicitor General's Office. This move completely removes the independence and compromises the integrity of the ombudsman. I would never work to destroy an office we worked so hard to build."

DISCUSSION QUESTIONS

1. To what extent should a politically appointed chief executive be free to restructure an agency?
2. How much input should the public have in areas that involve highly complex technical expertise? Should agencies be required to engage in formal rulemaking and/or adjudication before undertaking the type of action described in this case?
3. Based on the level of risk involved in these types of cases, should there be prospective judicial review? Should judicial review be available for any and all agencies' decisions?
4. Was Roberto Martinez constructively discharged? Did the executive director act in an ethically responsible manner?

CASE 66: NORTHERN SPOTTED OWL

The northern spotted owl is a species indigenous to North America. Its habitat is primarily old-growth forests of the U.S. Pacific Northwest and southern parts of British Columbia, Canada. In the 1970s and 1980s, a majority of the old-growth forests in the United States were on public lands that were open to logging. The owl's habitat shrank significantly.

In the state of Washington, the Department of Fish and Wildlife (DFW) is charged with managing the state's wildlife resources, including protection of species habitats. A number of environmental groups began to pressure the department to undertake greater protection of what little remained of the owl's habitat.

In response to environmentalists, the DFW undertook a scientific analysis of the owl's status and assigned a group of the agency's biologists to study the issue. Among the team members was Dr. Paul Billingsley, the DFW's expert on population viability. He concluded in a written research report, "The most reasonable interpretation of current data and knowledge indicates continued old-growth harvesting is likely to lead to the extinction of the northern spotted owl in the state of Washington, which argues strongly for providing greater protection to the state's old-growth forests."

The DFW had Dr. Billingsley's analysis peer reviewed by a number of other experts. Some of the experts had some criticism of Dr. Billingsley's work; however, ultimately, all the reviewers agreed with his conclusions.

A number of powerful logging companies found out about the department's study and began to complain to state legislators and the department, that any action on the part of the department would have a serious economic impact on not only their businesses, but the state economy as a whole.

Later in the year, the DFW concluded its review and decided that it would not increase protection of the identified forests. DFW provided almost no rationale for the basis of the decision. A number of environmental groups brought suit against the department in state superior court.

After a bench trial, Superior Court Judge Kevin Lair stated in his order that, "The Department of Fish and Wildlife has acted in total disregard of its own scientific findings. Therefore, the plaintiff's request for mandamus is granted and the case is remanded back to the department. The department is to reevaluate its decision and develop a plan for protection of the owl."

DISCUSSION QUESTIONS

1. How extensively should administrative agencies be required to justify decisions made within the scope of their expertise?
2. If you were a decision maker at DFW, how would you resolve the conflict between the two very compelling interests of economic vitality and environmental protection? How would you go about balancing these values? Which value do you think should prevail? Justify your answer.
3. After the court's extensive review of the scientific findings, should it simply have ordered the DFW to prohibit all logging in the state's old-growth forests? Why or why not?
4. The major decisions in this case were made by public administrators and judges. Examine the role of the legislature in this case. Should it have taken a more active role and if so, in what direction?

CASE 67: FUNDING THE FROG STUDY

Herbert Kraft was in the congressional staff room listening to his own Senator Tammy Wallis speak in favor of the university research bill. It had just passed out of Wallis's own committee. Herbert then did a double take. "What did he just say?"

"I don't know . . . I wasn't listening," said Liana Munn, another one of the Wallis staffers.

"I think he's trying to kill the frog study." Herbert then turned up the volume on C-SPAN.

"As my constituents know, I am a firm believer in investing in science and technology," Wallis said as she then picked up a small bundle of papers for theatrical effect. "But I just found out that the opposition party has just tried to use the amendment process to sneak into this high priority bill some needless pork. What is it you may ask? Here in the midst of valuable dollars that we'll be spending on the future of our technological infrastructure . . . in the midst of valuable dollars that will be spent on appropriate responses to climate change . . . in the midst of valuable dollars slated to be spent to cure the most dread diseases of mankind, what do we find? We find a worthless, wasteful $40,000 research grant to study frogs in South Carolina. I like Kermit as much as anybody, but this is ridiculous. Where are our priorities? I urge my fellow senators to beat down this pet project that my good ol' friends Senators Lansing and Weaver of South Carolina have tried to slip past. Don't they have a research triangle there? If they need to spread around some local dollars, let's spend it on that."

Herbert turned down the volume. "That's North Carolina," an exasperated Herbert whispered under his breath. "The research triangle is in *North* Carolina. What is she doing? We talked about this."

"Why are you so upset about her getting a state wrong?" asked Liana.

"I'm not upset about her confusing North and South Carolina. Before I came to DC, I used to think there was a West and an *East* Virginia. The problem is that her so-called frog study is going to be used to help deal with climate change and with medical research. I can't believe she forgot that—we just talked about that specifically this morning. I mean . . . she's the one who asked me to look into it."

Liana looked perplexed. "I don't see how a study on frogs is going to help deal with climate change or medical research."

"Frogs are like canaries in a coal mine. We're seeing massive die-offs and mutations worldwide. Some scientists think it's runoff pollution from agriculture and others think there might be a link to global warming. We've also made a lot of progress toward treating numerous diseases using the unique chemistry of amphibians as a source of research. The money spent on the South Carolina frog study is going to pay off great dividends—that is if our lovely and gracious senator hasn't killed it for good."

Just then Senator Wallis peaked in the door. "Liana, Herbert, . . . what did you think of my performance?"

Herbert jumped right in. "Senator, with all due respect, I think you just killed a very worthwhile program by slamming the frog study like that. I thought you understood. I did all the background research and I briefed you this morning. You asked a lot of good questions. I thought you got it."

"I got it. You need to remember that I've got a tough race coming up and my conservative opponent is going to lambaste me for wasteful spending. What you saw on the floor there is my next campaign commercial. It's going to portray me as a watchdog for the taxpayers' money. If the amendment gets voted down, we'll get it passed again next year. You have to understand Herbert, that in my line of work, what is right and what looks right are often two different things. I can do better for my constituents in the long run, especially in matters of health policy and the environment, if I get to stay in office. In order to stay in office in our conservative state, I have to know when to bend a little. Stay in this town a little longer and you'll begin to understand too. In the meantime, I need you to begin finding information for me on fertilizers and herbicides used on suburban turf—you know backyards and golf courses. Thanks!"

DISCUSSION QUESTIONS

1. Is Senator Wallis engaging in hypocrisy by slamming the frog study? Is Senator Wallis right in commenting that in politics "what is right and what looks right are often two different things"?
2. Have Senator Wallis's political maneuverings created special challenges for leading her own staff members? Has she explained her rationale to Herbert sufficiently so that he will remain an effective researcher and source of staff support for her?
3. What are the risks involved when politicians employ tactics like Wallis's floor speech? Are there better ways to accomplish her goals?
4. What should Herbert do about his misgivings? Are there any ethical principles that can provide guidance or perspective to him as he sorts out the priorities and actions of Senator Wallis?

CASE 68: PENCILING IN YOUR OWN SALARY

After six years in the basement at the Department of Environmental Regulation (DER), Zach finally broke through. His second interview for the position in Grants and Contracts went well, he thought, and it seems he was correct. With his favorite green push pins, Zach posted the letter from Human Resources on his cubicle wall.

"Grant Manager, Level 2," Zach read aloud. Just then Tiki, his supervisor, tapped him on the shoulder.

"Congratulations Zach," said Tiki. "I had a feeling they'd give you the nod. Now don't you make me look bad up there, son. I gave you my highest recommendation."

"Don't worry," Zach replied. "I take my job very seriously."

The first week at the new job went well. Zach liked his new office, and window, just a bit more than his basement cubicle. He also looked forward to the first paycheck at his new rate—a 50 percent increase! And there was a pleasant surprise to boot. Stephanie Ortiz, an old friend from college, was given the job of training Zach in his new duties. Zach and Stephanie had always gotten along well, and Zach still wondered if there might be some real chemistry there. Yes, everything seemed wonderful, and Zach and Stephanie would interview a prospective grantee together later in the afternoon.

When Zach arrived in the conference room, Stephanie was already there. So was Professor Albee Commons, the prospective grantee.

"I'm happy to meet you, Professor," said Zach as Stephanie slid the grant application across to him. "Stephanie tells me your work on water-borne toxins is legendary."

"Oh," replied Commons, "I wouldn't go that far. But I am excited about this new project at the reservoir. My wife has been in and out of hospitals the last two years, and I've really missed working with DER. Tell me, Zach, do you have any questions for me?"

"Actually, Professor, I'm still kind of new here," said Zach. "I thought I would just take notes while you and Stephanie go through the proposal." But Zach did have one question he was keeping to himself. The proposal called for bi-weekly testing of samples from the reservoir and a brief report at the end of the year. To Zach's surprise, however, the budget narrative called for DER to pay Commons half of his annual salary. Zach did not understand how the project could take up that much of the Professor's time. After the meeting, Stephanie and Zach went through their checklist. Stephanie recommended approval, and asked Zach what he thought.

"Well, I'll go along with whatever you think," he said, "but I do have a question. Why are we paying half of his salary? That seems out of whack for a little project like this." Stephanie put down her pen, took a sip of coffee, and rolled her eyes.

"Okay, so, you realize that we don't actually pay the professor, right," she began. "He gets relieved of half his duties at the university, but he gets paid his usual salary and we reimburse the university for half. That's how these work."

"Right," Zach answered, "I get that part. But why are we paying for *half* of his time? This project won't even take a tenth of his time. Is that how it normally works?"

Stephanie explained further. "No, it doesn't normally work this way; but DER has had a long and productive relationship with Professor Commons. We rely on his testimony at administrative hearings, and he has always made time for us when we needed him. You know, Zach, these last two years have been really tough on him. He told you his wife had been in and out of hospitals, but he didn't mention that she died of cancer last Christmas. He's a wonderful man and he's been through so much. We are all just trying to help him get back to a normal life. Personally, I don't think it's such a bad idea to help him along with a nice, doable project like this. The man needs a little TLC, don't you think?"

DISCUSSION QUESTIONS

1. Evaluate the relationship between Stephanie Ortiz and Albee Commons. What is the appropriate role for Stephanie in this grant approval process? Why did the professor feel comfortable overstating his time commitment in the budget narrative?

2. Put yourself in Zach's shoes. Is he too new to object? To whom would he go with his objection? Does he feel any pressure to appease Stephanie? What, if anything, would you say to Stephanie?

3. Assume Zach keeps his objection to himself. Would that mean that Tiki's confidence in Zach was unjustified? If Zach really takes his job "very seriously" as he claims, what should he do? Do Stephanie and Albee have any reason to be concerned or worried?

4. Many attorneys and other professionals are paid on retainer, that is they accept compensation with the commitment to provide services when needed. Since the professor provides expert testimony at administrative hearings, could his salary be justified by some other means than time on task?

CASE 69: CARBON FOOTPRINT OF A GLOBAL WARMING ACTIVIST

Scott Lanier was just playing around with a couple of his friends from high school. While sitting in the passenger seat of a car at a local fast-food drive-in, Scott started to lip sync to a song blasting from the stereo. While doing so, his friend Jackie was sitting in the backseat videotaping his impromptu performance. It was a spur of the moment thing—the very kind of spontaneous outburst of wackiness that made Scott such an endearing and popular friend. Later, Jackie posted her video on her social networking site and also on YouTube. For some inexplicable reason, Scott's performance really caught on and became for a time one of the most popular performances on the Web. Little did he know how much his lip-syncing exhibition would change his life.

The call came just four months later while Scott was packing to go to college. He planned to major in the biological sciences with a minor in environmental studies.

"Thanks for taking my call Scott, and let me introduce myself. My name is Larry Benton and I'm with the Robbins & Martin Creative Talents Agency."

"Uh, yes sir, what can I do for you?" asked Scott.

"We would like to fly you out here to Los Angeles later this week. My associates are interested in getting to know you a bit better. We want to see if you're a good fit for our agency to represent in the entertainment industry. You see, we all got a kick out of your video and we think you might have some potential. It's easy. We'd just ask you to read through a few lines and do some work on film so that we can see how focus groups react to you. If things work out, we would use the considerable prestige of our agency to get you work on TV shows. In other words, we would help you manage your career and protect your interests. Would you be interested?"

"Wow! Sure, what do I need to do?"

"Well, just board a plane on Friday and come on out here. You'll have no out-of-pocket expenses—we'll feed you and put you up in a hotel and rent you a car and fly you out here and back. If this doesn't work out for either of us, you'll basically have had a nice vacation adventure at our expense and you can tell everybody you know about us California crazies. What do you say?"

Scott hesitated for a moment. He was excited about college and knew that this would cut into his first week. Then again, how many times in your life do you get a call like this? "Thanks, Mr. Benton? I'd love to."

Scott did it and it was the stereotypical Hollywood dream—first unexpected discovery, then stardom. Scott's first gig was on a TV series which ran four seasons. When his contract was over, the Robbins & Martin Agency scored him lead roles in three major motion pictures—all turned out to be incredibly popular comedies.

As one of the world's best known celebrities, Scott started to lend his name to various social causes and humanitarian efforts. Over time, he became most closely associated with the concern over climate change. He had participated in a music video that championed controlling the emissions of greenhouse gases in an effort to ward off global warming. Every time he guested on late-night TV talk shows, he was sure to bring up this topic and urge everyone to support alternative energies, to use compact fluorescent light bulbs, and to minimize their own energy use. He preached a lifestyle of simplicity. His proudest moment was when a documentary that featured his crusade against global warming won an Academy Award.

Scott had used some of the money he earned to buy a mansion just outside of Santa Fe, New Mexico where he spent most of his free time entertaining friends and courting his fiancé. To make his own home more "green" he installed numerous solar panels around his house and property. He started investing in technologies that take advantage of renewable resources. He bought "carbon credits" as a means to offset his own carbon footprint. In effect, he paid a third party to take actions such as planting trees to reduce the impact of greenhouse gases. He also traded in his large SUV for a new hybrid SUV that got considerably better gas mileage.

One of the most exciting bits of news that Scott was able to share with his family was his invitation to be a guest on a serious Sunday morning news talk show, the kind his dad always liked to watch. On that Sunday morning when he made his appearance, his father was beaming with pride.

"Everyone knows our next guest. He is one of the most popular entertainers on the world stage today. Scott Lanier is best known for his long-running hit TV show and he'll soon be appearing in his fourth major motion picture due out this summer. What people may not know about Mr. Lanier is his philanthropic work, especially the Lanier Family Foundation which was established just this year in order to promote energy conservation awareness. Thanks for coming to talk with us this morning, Scott."

"Thank you for having me." Scott then described in depth his concerns about the planet and offered several ways that people could do their part to limit global warming such as participating in recycling efforts, driving smaller cars that employ hybrid technologies, getting better insulation for houses, using mass transit, and simply walking more.

"Scott, I have here a report from the New Mexico Policy Research Center, a conservative think tank in Albuquerque." The moderator held up the slim volume. "Have you had a chance to read this yet?"

"No, I don't even know what it is."

"Let me share with you and our audience some of what it says." The screen behind them flashed excerpts from the report as the moderator read it aloud. "In the Santa Fe area, the most profligate energy hog is a large 8,900-square foot mansion on the side of a hill on the southeast side of town. The house consumes twenty-five times the national average in terms of electricity. In this dry part of the country, the house uses several thousands of gallons of water per year to keep the golf-course-quality turf around the house green and lush. That house is owned by none other than famed environmental advocate, Scott Lanier."

"Hey, let me respond to that," said Scott as he tried to gather his thoughts. "First of all, I have that water trucked in so I'm not using the municipal water supply. And a lot of my electricity is powered by solar panels and I buy carbon credits to offset my carbon footprint."

"How many houses do you own?"

"Uh . . . I'm not sure."

"You don't even know how many houses you own?"

"It's kind of complicated. Let's see I have a house in Burbank which I often use while filming . . . uh, and of course my home in New Mexico. I also have several investment properties, . . . but I hire someone to manage those. There's an apartment I rent in New York City and a condo in Aspen. Actually, none of this is your business. That's as rude as asking a rancher how many cows he owns."

"Speaking of cows, Scott . . . do you eat meat?"

"You know, I admit to being a carnivore. That was how I was raised, but I do try to eat meat that is free of antibiotics and hormones."

The moderator interrupted. "You realize, Scott, that some of the publications from your own foundation recommend moving away from meat as a major supply of protein since cattle flatulence is thought to contribute to global warming."

"Really? Yeah, I guess. I never said that I was perfect, but I am trying to do my part."

"Scott, how did you get to Washington, DC to appear on this show?"

"I flew."

"Did you take a commercial flight?"

"No, I used a private jet service. I see where you're going with this, but you have to understand that I have major commitments for my time and I often have to be in various locations for filming and guest appearances like this. It's how I do my work and it's also how I spread the warning against global warming."

"Scott, thanks so much for being with us this morning. We hope you come back soon, and good luck with your movie this summer."

DISCUSSION QUESTIONS

1. Is Scott's behavior "green" enough to square with his commitment to the environment? What principles are relevant? Are there any ethical principles that would separate Scott's personal behavior from his strident public advocacy of environmentalism?

2. Does someone's inability to live up to their own high standards call into question the rightness of the standards themselves?

3. Is it an effective strategy for the New Mexico Policy Research Center to attack the messenger instead of the message? Is it an ethical strategy? Why or why not?

4. Could Scott have done more to help the environment by going to college and studying fields related to the environment rather than cultivating a career in the entertainment business? Explain.

APPENDIX

Cases Listed by Subject Areas

AFFIRMATIVE ACTION
- Case 55: The Fair Employment Practices Act

BENEFITS ADMINISTRATION
- Case 14: Tuition Reimbursement Program

BUDGET MANAGEMENT
- Case 13: The Long Forgotten Raise in the Property Tax
- Case 22: Maintaining Pay during Reduction in Force

BUREAUCRATIC DISCRETION
- Case 55: The Fair Employment Practices Act

CITY COUNCIL
- Case 7: Gay Rights Signs on City Utility Poles
- Case 8: Serving at the Pleasure of the City Council
- Case 15: Submitting an Incomplete Financial Report
- Case 21: Selecting the Special Assistant to the City Council
- Case 44: Pornography and the Police Chief's Wife
- Case 48: Records Check

CIVIL LIBERTIES

- Case 40: State University Football Coach and the Wayward Team
- Case 44: Pornography and the Police Chief's Wife
- Case 58: Hate Speech in Confidential Course Evaluations

COMPENSATION

- Case 22: Maintaining Pay during Reduction in Force
- Case 23: A Speed Bump on Staff
- Case 41: Working Extra to Pay Your Own Salary
- Case 59: Equal Pay Experts in a Hot Tub
- Case 68: Penciling in Your Own Salary

DIVERSITY ISSUES AND MANAGEMENT

- Case 7: Gay Rights Signs on City Utility Poles
- Case 14: Tuition Reimbursement Program
- Case 21: Selecting the Special Assistant to the City Council
- Case 23: A Speed Bump on Staff
- Case 24: The Bureaucrat's Wife
- Case 37: Changing the Grade
- Case 48: Records Check
- Case 51: American General Opines on Gays
- Case 54: Sensitivity Training and Pandora's Box
- Case 55: The Fair Employment Practices Act
- Case 56: Weekend Racist
- Case 57: Accommodating a Student with a Disability
- Case 58: Hate Speech in Confidential Course Evaluations
- Case 59: Equal Pay Experts in a Hot Tub

ECONOMIC DEVELOPMENT

- Case 31: Tourism Advertisement
- Case 32: A Reasonable Offer
- Case 33: Shootout at the Zoning Commission: MegaStore v. the Pharmacists
- Case 34: Complimentary Soda Drinks for Bus Drivers
- Case 35: The Ethanol Loan Subsidy
- Case 36: Free Building for Titan Trout Shop
- Case 50: Indecent Exposure and the Board of Cosmetology
- Case 61: Ghost Worker at the Nonprofit
- Case 66: Northern Spotted Owl

EDUCATION

EMERGENCY MANAGEMENT

EMPLOYEE RELATIONS

ENVIRONMENTAL PROTECTION

EQUAL EMPLOYMENT OPPORTUNITY

ETHICS

- Case 2: Not Paying Taxes at the IRS
- Case 4: Eleven Months to Retirement
- Case 9: Office of Emergency Management Fake Press Conference
- Case 11: The Governor's Transition Team
- Case 12: Running the Numbers at the State Health Department
- Case 15: Submitting an Incomplete Financial Report
- Case 17: Free Boat for Soda Display at State Lodge
- Case 20: Patronage Charges against the Governor
- Case 24: The Bureaucrat's Wife
- Case 25: Pennies from Heaven
- Case 26: Spanking the Foster Child
- Case 30: Privatizing the County Hospital
- Case 31: Tourism Advertisement
- Case 32: A Reasonable Offer
- Case 35: The Ethanol Loan Subsidy
- Case 36: Free Building for Titan Trout Shop
- Case 37: Changing the Grade
- Case 38: The Superintendent's Scandal
- Case 39: Gift Certificate for Recommendation Letter
- Case 43: Rough Day in Tornado Alley
- Case 48: Records Check
- Case 53: Advertisement for Topless Bar in University Newspaper
- Case 56: Weekend Racist
- Case 63: University President Protests Football Official's Decision
- Case 68: Penciling in Your Own Salary

FAMILY-FRIENDLY POLICIES

- Case 2: Not Paying Taxes at the IRS
- Case 24: The Bureaucrat's Wife

FEDERAL GOVERNMENT

- Case 2: Not Paying Taxes at the IRS
- Case 6: A Termination by Any Other Name
- Case 24: The Bureaucrat's Wife
- Case 45: Nukes Travel Cross County
- Case 47: Cyber Terrorism
- Case 51: American General Opines on Gays

FINANCIAL MANAGEMENT

- Case 11: The Governor's Transition Team
- Case 13: The Long Forgotten Raise in the Property Tax

GRANTS

HUMAN RESOURCES

INFORMATION TECHNOLOGY AND MANAGEMENT

- Case 47: Cyber Terrorism
- Case 56: Weekend Racist

INTEREST GROUPS

- Case 7: Gay Rights Signs on City Utility Poles
- Case 61: Ghost Worker at the Nonprofit
- Case 62: Sharing the Donor List
- Case 66: Northern Spotted Owl
- Case 69: Carbon Footprint of a Global Warming Activist

INTERGOVERNMENTAL RELATIONS

- Case 9: Office of Emergency Management Fake Press Conference
- Case 29: Prenatal Care for Illegal Immigrants
- Case 45: Nukes Travel Cross County
- Case 48: Records Check
- Case 55: The Fair Employment Practices Act
- Case 59: Equal Pay Experts in a Hot Tub
- Case 68: Penciling in Your Own Salary

LABOR RELATIONS

- Case 3: Cutting Loose the Dirty Dozen
- Case 10: Squeezing Out the Garbage Collectors
- Case 14: Tuition Reimbursement Program

LEGAL ISSUES

- Case 13: The Long Forgotten Raise in the Property Tax
- Case 18: Charging for Copies of Public Documents
- Case 20: Patronage Charges against the Governor
- Case 22: Maintaining Pay during Reduction in Force
- Case 26: Spanking the Foster Child
- Case 29: Prenatal Care for Illegal Immigrants
- Case 31: Tourism Advertisement
- Case 52: Hollywood Discovery
- Case 55: The Fair Employment Practices Act
- Case 58: Hate Speech in Confidential Course Evaluations
- Case 66: Northern Spotted Owl

LOCAL GOVERNMENT

- Case 3: Cutting Loose the Dirty Dozen
- Case 5: A Competent but Slow Employee
- Case 8: Serving at the Pleasure of the City Council
- Case 10: Squeezing Out the Garbage Collectors
- Case 13: The Long Forgotten Raise in the Property Tax
- Case 18: Charging for Copies of Public Documents
- Case 22: Maintaining Pay during Reduction in Force
- Case 30: Privatizing the County Hospital
- Case 36: Free Building for Titan Trout Shop
- Case 38: The Superintendent's Scandal
- Case 43: Rough Day in Tornado Alley
- Case 48: Records Check
- Case 60: Firefighters Get Money for Charity

MANAGING EMPLOYEES

- Case 1: Floggings Will Continue
- Case 2: Not Paying Taxes at the IRS
- Case 3: Cutting Loose the Dirty Dozen
- Case 5: A Competent but Slow Employee
- Case 6: A Termination by Any Other Name
- Case 8: Serving at the Pleasure of the City Council
- Case 12: Running the Numbers at the State Health Department
- Case 16: Ineligible for Suggestion System Awards
- Case 20: Patronage Charges against the Governor
- Case 22: Maintaining Pay during Reduction in Force
- Case 23: A Speed Bump on Staff
- Case 25: Pennies from Heaven
- Case 27: Children Abused in State Institution
- Case 28: Smoking at the State Health Department
- Case 40: State University Football Coach and the Wayward Team

MILITARY

- Case 45: Nukes Travel Cross County
- Case 51: American General Opines on Gays

NONPROFIT MANAGEMENT

- Case 46: Highway Patrol Officer Sells Benefit Tickets
- Case 60: Firefighters Get Money for Charity
- Case 61: Ghost Worker at the Nonprofit
- Case 62: Sharing the Donor List

- Case 63: University President Protests Football Official's Decision
- Case 64: The Lazy Volunteer
- Case 69: Carbon Footprint of a Global Warming Activist

OVERSIGHT

- Case 20: Patronage Charges against the Governor
- Case 28: Smoking at the State Health Department
- Case 29: Prenatal Care for Illegal Immigrants
- Case 34: Complimentary Soda Drinks for Bus Drivers
- Case 35: The Ethanol Loan Subsidy
- Case 49: The Corrections Officer Selection Video
- Case 61: Ghost Worker at the Nonprofit
- Case 65: An Ombudsman by Any Other Name
- Case 67: Funding the Frog Study

PLANNING

- Case 19: The Planning Director and the HR Analyst
- Case 32: A Reasonable Offer
- Case 33: Shootout at the Zoning Commission: MegaStore v. the Pharmacists
- Case 36: Free Building for Titan Trout Shop

POLITICAL CAMPAIGN

- Case 20: Patronage Charges against the Governor
- Case 67: Funding the Frog Study

POLITICAL PATRONAGE

- Case 11: The Governor's Transition Team
- Case 20: Patronage Charges against the Governor
- Case 24: The Bureaucrat's Wife

POLITICS/ADMINISTRATION DICHOTOMY

- Case 2: Not Paying Taxes at the IRS
- Case 8: Serving at the Pleasure of the City Council
- Case 11: The Governor's Transition Team
- Case 19: The Planning Director and the HR Analyst
- Case 20: Patronage Charges against the Governor
- Case 21: Selecting the Special Assistant to the City Council
- Case 24: The Bureaucrat's Wife

- Case 7: Gay Rights Signs on City Utility Poles
- Case 9: Office of Emergency Management Fake Press Conference
- Case 11: The Governor's Transition Team
- Case 13: The Long Forgotten Raise in the Property Tax
- Case 14: Tuition Reimbursement Program
- Case 18: Charging for Copies of Public Documents
- Case 20: Patronage Charges against the Governor
- Case 24: The Bureaucrat's Wife
- Case 27: Children Abused in State Institution
- Case 28: Smoking at the State Health Department
- Case 29: Prenatal Care for Illegal Immigrants
- Case 31: Tourism Advertisement
- Case 34: Complimentary Soda Drinks for Bus Drivers
- Case 38: The Superintendent's Scandal
- Case 40: State University Football Coach and the Wayward Team
- Case 44: Pornography and the Police Chief's Wife
- Case 45: Nukes Travel Cross County
- Case 49: The Corrections Officer Selection Video
- Case 50: Indecent Exposure and the Board of Cosmetology
- Case 51: American General Opines on Gays
- Case 52: Hollywood Discovery
- Case 53: Advertisement for Topless Bar in University Newspaper
- Case 63: University President Protests Football Official's Decision
- Case 69: Carbon Footprint of a Global Warming Activist

PURCHASING AND PROCUREMENT

- Case 8: Serving at the Pleasure of the City Council
- Case 17: Free Boat for Soda Display at State Lodge
- Case 31: Tourism Advertisement
- Case 38: The Superintendent's Scandal

SEXUAL HARASSMENT

- Case 42: Professor Dating Student

SOCIAL WELFARE

- Case 25: Pennies from Heaven
- Case 26: Spanking the Foster Child
- Case 27: Children Abused in State Institution
- Case 29: Prenatal Care for Illegal Immigrants
- Case 48: Records Check

TAXES

- Case 2: Not Paying Taxes at the IRS
- Case 13: The Long Forgotten Raise in the Property Tax

TOURISM

- Case 17: Free Boat for Soda Display at State Lodge
- Case 31: Tourism Advertisement
- Case 33: Shootout at the Zoning Commission: MegaStore v. the Pharmacists
- Case 34: Complimentary Soda Drinks for Bus Drivers

TRAINING AND DEVELOPMENT

- Case 14: Tuition Reimbursement Program
- Case 49: The Corrections Officer Selection Video

TRANSPORTATION

- Case 6: A Termination by Any Other Name
- Case 32: A Reasonable Offer
- Case 69: Carbon Footprint of a Global Warming Activist

URBAN MANAGEMENT

- Case 8: Serving at the Pleasure of the City Council
- Case 13: The Long Forgotten Raise in the Property Tax
- Case 18: Charging for Copies of Public Documents
- Case 19: The Planning Director and the HR Analyst
- Case 22: Maintaining Pay during Reduction in Force

WHISTLEBLOWING

- Case 11: The Governor's Transition Team
- Case 38: The Superintendent's Scandal
- Case 45: Nukes Travel Cross County